FAMOUS
Love
Letters

A READER'S DIGEST BOOK

Produced by Andromeda Oxford Ltd.

The acknowledgments that appear on
page 154 are hereby made a part of
this copyright page.

Library of Congress Cataloging in Publication Data

Famous love letters : messages of intimacy and passion / edited by
    Ronald Tamplin.
        p.   cm.
    Includes bibliographical references and index.
    ISBN 0-89577-649-9
    1. Love letters. 2. Celebrities—Correspondence. I. Tamplin,
Ronald. II. Reader's Digest Association.
PN6140.L7F33 1995
808.6'9354—dc20

                                                    94-31063

Printed in Spain

FAMOUS
Love Letters

MESSAGES OF INTIMACY AND PASSION

Edited by Ronald Tamplin

THE READER'S DIGEST ASSOCIATION, INC.
Pleasantville, New York/Montreal

"There is only one situation

I can think of

in which men and women

make an effort to read

better than they usually do.

[It is] when they are in love

and reading a love letter."

MORTIMER ADLER
December 1961.

Contents

Introduction

Throughout history lovers have tried to capture in letters the elusive quality of love. Born out of separation—whether for just a few hours or for many years—love letters capture the most intimate feelings of the sender. Reading the words of lovers allows us to enter into the drama of their emotions, to share the idiosyncrasies and universalities of their passions.

The love letters of the world range from blunt and artless expressions—such as Peter Withers's moving letter to his wife immediately prior to his banishment to Australia in 1830—to the effusions of some of history's greatest writers, artists, and musicians. The loves of the well-known, including Henry IV of France for Gabrielle d'Estrées in the 1590's, and Napoleon for Josephine two hundred years later, can literally change history. It is no wonder that the lives and loves of the past, as well as the present, continue to fascinate us.

The experience of every individual is unique, but some things in love never change. There have always been lovers who experienced the lightning bolt of love at first sight: Lord Randolph Churchill proposed to Jennie Jerome in 1873 after just one evening spent together at a society ball. Others, such as Fanny Kemble and Pierce Butler, have given themselves to a whirlwind romance before making the momentous decision to marry. Some lovers have shown through their letters constancy and devotion in the face of insuperable odds, whether war, sickness, separation, or determined opposition of family and society. Mozart defied the wishes of his whole family to marry Constanze Weber; Anton Chekhov fought against illness and his own sense of isolation to marry the actress Olga Knipper; and Arctic explorer Robert Peary remained devoted to his wife Josephine during long years of separation.

Letters have been used to declare undying love; to ask for the hand (or the body) of the beloved; to reject unwanted suitors; to express jealousies and to challenge the betrayals (real or imagined) of the loved one. Even after the height of passion has faded, letters have communicated a deep and enduring love, as Sophia Peabody demonstrated in her letter to her husband Nathaniel Hawthorne in 1839. Other lovers, such as composer Leoš Janáček and writer Franz Kafka, have poured out their frustrated wishes to their loved ones. And in the last moments of life, letters have been used to recall the deepest passions of a lifetime, as in Catherine of Aragon's moving and dignified farewell letter to Henry VIII.

This book contains 34 love letters collected from all over the world, dating from Roman times to the 20th century. The letters give us the opportunity to meet men and women in their most unguarded moments, displaying in a manner unique to themselves feelings that are familiar to us all. Each letter highlights a particularly poignant moment from a love story. The lovers who wrote the letters crystallize emotions that we all live daily. Reading their words is to recreate both them and us.

Love Down the Ages

"... Love can be understood

only 'from the inside,'

as a language can be understood

only by someone who speaks it,

as a world can be understood

only by someone

who lives in it."

ROBERT C. SOLOMON,
Love: Emotion, Myth and Metaphor

Ovid to his wife

c. A.D. 8–17

I plowed the vast ocean on a frail bit of timber; [whereas] the ship that bore the son of Æson [Jason]* was strong....The furtive arts of Cupid aided him; arts which I wish that Love had not learned from me. He returned home; I shall die in these lands, if the heavy wrath of the offended God shall be lasting. My burden, most faithful wife, is a harder one than that which the son of Æson bore. You, too, whom I left still young at my departure from the City, I can believe to have grown old under my calamities. Oh, grant it, ye Gods, that I may be enabled to see you, even if such, and to give the joyous kiss on each cheek in its turn; and to embrace your emaciated body in my arms, and to say, "'twas anxiety, on my account, that caused this thinness"; and, weeping, to recount in person my sorrows to you in tears, and thus enjoy a conversation that I had never hoped for; and to offer the due frankincense, with grateful hand, to the Caesars, and to the wife that is worthy of a Caesar, Deities in real truth!

Oh, that the mother of Memnon, that Prince being softened, would with her rosy lips, speedily call forth that day.

Above *A "frail bit of timber" carried Ovid across rough seas to his nine-year exile in Tomis. This marble relief from a second-century* A.D. *sarcophagus conjures up the scene.*

* Ovid compares his sea-journey into exile with the voyage made by Jason and the Argonauts, who went in search of the legendary Golden Fleece. He laments the fact that his own troubles are far worse than those Jason experienced.

The Roman poet Ovid, born in 43 B.C., wrote his best work during the reign of the emperor Augustus. Little is known about his third wife, a woman he truly loved and from whom he was separated forever when he was sent into exile. But his many letters to her, including the one extracted here—written in the form of public appeals to raise sympathy for his release—provide an insight into some of the earliest surviving "love letters."

Exactly why Augustus ordered the most famous poet of the time into exile is not known. But there is no doubt that Ovid's sophisticated handbook on the art of pursuing another man's wife—his poem *The Art of Love* (*Ars amatoria*; published in about 1 B.C.)—would have made the emperor extremely angry. Augustus was determined to transform the scandalous morals of Roman society, and to this end passed laws inflicting severe penalties on adulterous couples. He had even banished his own daughter, Julia, from Rome—a woman notorious for her adulterous affairs—as an example to others.

Exile to distant and usually unpleasant parts of the Roman Empire was a regular punishment in ancient Rome, and this happened to the 51-year-old Ovid in the winter of A.D. 8. He was sentenced to live in Tomis (present-day Constanta), then a bleak spot near the mouth of the Danube River in Romania. The rough sea passage by ship across the Mediterranean and Black Sea left him with bitter memories. His letters from exile to friends and dignitaries made it very clear that he always hoped to be granted a reprieve by the emperor. Meanwhile, back in Rome his third wife devoted her time to campaigning hard for his release and the protection of his property.

A valuable piece of first-hand information about Ovid's three wives comes from a few lines in his *Sorrows* (*Tristia*), five books of poems that he wrote during the early years of his exile (c. A.D. 8–12):

Above *A bust of the Roman poet Ovid (43 B.C.–A.D. 17), who was suddenly sent into exile by the emperor Augustus, separating him from his wife in Rome. They wrote to each other throughout Ovid's nine-year exile until his death, always in the hope that they would be reunited.*

Right *Lines from Book Four of Ovid's Letters from the Black Sea, from an 8th- or 9th-century codex in Hamburg. His letter to his wife, extracted opposite, is another of the Black Sea letters.*

"I was hardly more than a boy when I was given a wife, unworthy and useless; the marriage lasted only for a short time. To her succeeded another, and she was blameless, but she was not to remain in union with me. The last, who has stayed with me throughout the many years, had the courage to be an exile's wife."

Like so many of Rome's best writers, Ovid came originally from the provinces. He decided at an early age that he was going to be a poet. Although poetry played an important part in Roman life—used as a medium to teach moral lessons—men with ambition went into business, farming, the army, or the law. The young Ovid's first marriage failed. There was an early divorce, and he then became a "man about town" in the society that emerged as Augustus brought peace and prosperity to Rome. His first poems, the *Loves* (*Amores*), were something new in Roman literature: a collection of verses that taught not the arts of war or statesmanship but the art of love and seduction. Here is how he treated the subject of love letters at this stage in his life, before his exile:

"If she asks how I am, say I live in longing. My letter provides all the details. Quick, do not let's waste time talking. Catch her at a free moment, give her the note—and make sure she reads it at once. Watch her face and eyes as she does so, expressions can be revealing of things to come. And take care she replies on the spot, with a good long letter. Half-blank tablets drive me mad, so get her to crowd up her lines, and fill the margins from side to side. But wait—Why should she weary her fingers with all that scribbling? One single word is good enough: 'Come.' Then I would wreath my victorious writing tablet with laurel, and hang it in Venus' shrine."

Exile was bitter for this sophisticated Roman. In Tomis, a semi-Hellenized port subject to attacks from surrounding barbarian tribes, little Latin was spoken and the climate was severe. The verse letters to his wife back in Rome—*Letters from the Black Sea (Epistulae ex Ponto)*, of which the letter extracted is one,

Right *A fresco from Herculaneum showing a self-indulgent young man reclining beside a courtesan. This was the kind of behavior Ovid wrote about in* The Art of Love. *In one poem he was critical of the bourgeois morality of Rome in Augustus' day, and it may be for this that he was exiled to Tomis.*

Below *Part of the Peutinger map, a medieval copy of a late Roman map of the empire, showing the position of Tomis (present-day Constanta, center right of map) at the mouth of the Danube, on the fringes of the empire.*

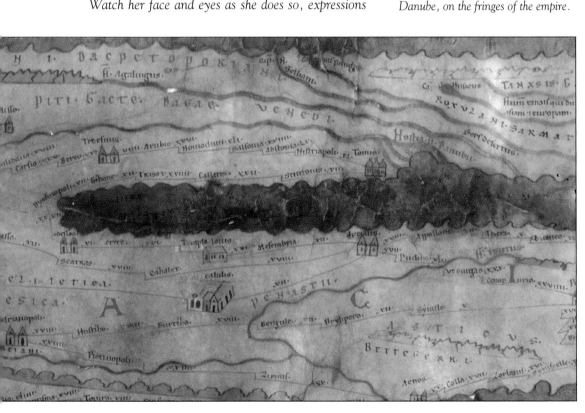

were written during the later years of his exile from c. A.D. 12 to 16. They were "public" poems intended to be seen by the emperor, in which Ovid movingly expressed his loneliness and feelings for his wife: love, sorrow at their separation, and guilt at doubting her constancy. He praised her virtues, and the fortitude of true love. In Elegy VI he wrote:

> *"Not so much was Lydè beloved by the poet of Claros...as you, my wife, are endeared to my heart....By you, as though a beam for my support, was my fall upheld."*

He thought of his wife receiving his letters:

> *"Do you turn pale when a fresh letter comes from Pontus, opening it with a trembling hand?"*

And in Elegy III, a letter in which he told her he had suffered ill health, he wrote:

> *"I am lying here worn out, among the remotest tribes and regions....And...you, my wife...occupy more than your equal share in my heart. My voice names you only; no night, no day comes to me without you...your name is ever on my wandering lips....Tears sometimes have the weight of words."*

Ovid died during his ninth year in exile, at the age of 60. His brilliant early poems captured the hearts and influenced the writing of later ages, but only in exile did the poet himself come to understand the full range and meaning of the subject with which he had been so long preoccupied: love.

The *Lovers*

PUBLIUS OVIDIUS NASO
(43 B.C.–A.D. 17)
wrote cool, witty, "modern" poems about the arts of love. Born in Sulmona, Italy, a small provincial town, he was educated in Rome and traveled in Greece before shocking and delighting Roman society with his poems, the *Loves* (*Amores*; written at intervals from 20 B.C. onward) and *The Art of Love* (*Ars amatoria*; c. 1 B.C.). Married three times, only his last marriage appears to have been a love match. Exiled to Tomis on the Black Sea for displeasing the emperor Augustus, he was separated from his wife until his death nine years later. His last and greatest work, the *Metamorphoses*, a collection of myths and legends that inspired many later writers, had just been completed when he was banished.

OVID'S WIFE
(dates and name unknown)
is known to history almost entirely through the verse letters that Ovid wrote her during their separation. She is thought to have been a widow at the time of their marriage and a member of the noble Fabian family. During his nine-year exile, she remained in Rome to administer his estates and to try to persuade their influential friends to intercede with the emperor for his release.

Ariwara no Narihira to the Imperial Princess

c. mid–ninth century

Princess

> I know not whether
> It was I who journeyed there
> Or you who came to me:
> Was it dream or reality?
> Was I sleeping or awake?

Narihira

> Last night I too
> Wandered lost in the darkness
> Of a disturbed heart
> Whether dream or reality
> Tonight let us decide!

Princess

> Shallow the inlet
> If the traveler wading it
> Is not even wetted

Narihira

> I shall cross again to you
> Over Meeting Barrier.

Above *Some of the verses of Ariwara no Narihira's poem reproduced in a 13th-century manuscript of the* Kokin Wakashu, *a poetry anthology originally commissioned by the imperial family in 905. This version is likely to have been written from memory rather than copied.*

Love letters have never been more important to the development of relationships between the sexes than they were in the courtly society of medieval Japan. The exchange printed here is taken from the ninth-century (Heian period) *Tales of Ise*, a largely autobiographical account of the love life of the imperial court poet and nobleman Ariwara no Narihira. Narihira's relationship with the imperial princess, a vestal virgin of the Great Shinto Shrine of Ise, was casual and of a sort quite common among members of the aristocracy. But such a relationship was treated with a delicacy alien to Western tradition, as Narihira's story illustrates.

Below *Japanese courtly love centered on the activity of writing poems and prose to one's lover, as the woman on the far right is doing. The screen dates from the Edo period (1603–1868), which saw a major revival of the Heian culture of Ariwara's day.*

Above *Ariwara no Narihira—nobleman, landowner, soldier, and imperial court poet—by the artist Kikuchi [Yōsai] Takeyasu. The 11th-century poet and critic Fujiwara Kinto hailed Narihira as one of Japan's "36 Poetical Geniuses."*

According to the *Tales of Ise*, the emperor sent Narihira as his envoy to the Ise Shrine; this was the holiest of Japan's sacred shrines, dedicated to the Sun Goddess, from whom the imperial family claimed descent. On his first night there the imperial princess gave him rooms in her own wing of the palace and attended to all his needs. No description of her has survived, but she probably followed the medieval Japanese ideas of beauty: a face of chalky powdered pallor; plucked and painted eyebrows; teeth that were blackened. She almost certainly had long, glossy black hair, which was thought particularly beautiful if it reached the ground. On the second night the princess, at Narihira's suggestion, came to him in the middle of the night and stayed with him until the third hour of the morning, when she was obliged to return to her own rooms. This was an acceptable practice because the Shinto religion laid down no moral code; its central theme was the joyful acceptance of the natural world and gratitude for its beauty.

The next day, as was customary, Narihira waited anxiously for her to send a verse letter by messenger. When it finally arrived, Narihira wept. In the culture of the time this was not a sign of weakness but of extreme sensibility to the beauty and pathos of life, and it was expected of the ideal Heian gentleman. Narihira wrote a verse in reply in which, like the princess's verse, dream and reality became as one.

On the third night, unexpectedly, circumstances kept the lovers apart, and the following morning Narihira had to leave. As dawn broke, a messenger arrived from the princess bearing a cup of parting. Inside it was written the princess's next verse:

> *"Shallow the inlet*
> *If the traveler wading it*
> *Is not even wetted."*

Narihira drank the wine from the cup and, using charcoal from a pinewood torch, added the last verse; he promised he would come back to her across the mountains, which were appropriately named Meeting Barrier. The exchange encapsulates all the elements of the aristocratic Japanese approach to love: power, refined expression, charm, and at the center a sense of sorrow at the heart of things.

Narihira and the princess lived in a highly ritualized society, in which the exchange of verses formed a central part of courtship. Every detail relating to the letter—the paper, the handwriting, and even the messenger—carried special significance and revealed the sensibility of the lovers. The paper had to be of the right thickness, color, and size to suit the emotional mood of the message. It had to be folded in the correct way and attached to a sprig of blossom, which would then be delivered by a handsome messenger. A "morning after" letter such as Narihira's poem was traditionally attached to a sprig from a pine tree, indicating to the lady that the sender's love—like the pine—would never wither. Narihira used pinewood charcoal instead of a sprig to write his reply inside the princess's wine cup.

Calligraphy was also important. An affair could founder if the man was disappointed by the woman's handwriting. And it was generally expected in courtly circles that anyone could produce, at a moment's notice, a poem to fit any occasion, especially an occasion of love.

Every aspect of a lover's behavior was ritualized. While it was quite acceptable for a Japanese aristocrat to have a "one-

Left *The inner shrine of the Great Shrine of Ise in southern Honshu, Japan. Dedicated to the Sun Goddess, it was presided over by a succession of imperial princesses including, in the mid–ninth century, Ariwara's lover.*

ARIWARA NO NARIHIRA
(823–880)
was the fifth son of Prince Aho and a grandson of the emperor Heijo. He and his brothers, on their father's advice, renounced their royal rank and became noblemen. Narihira owned estates near the former capital of Nara and held a succession of government offices. The year before he died, he was lieutenant general of the Left Division of the Imperial Guard. He is best known for his poetry, a major contribution to the culture of the Heian period (794–1185). His most famous work is the *Ise mono-gatari*, or *Tales of Ise*. A collection of his verse appeared in the *Kokin wakashu (Anthology of Poems Old and New)* compiled in 905 by the poet Ki no Tsurayuki. In the late 18th century—the Edo period—the Wakashu poets won renewed popularity as part of a Japanese revivalist movement.

THE IMPERIAL PRINCESS
(Name and dates unknown)
was an important guardian of the Great Shrine of Ise in southern Honshu. It was there that she had her brief affair with Ariwara no Narihira. The inner shrine of the Ise complex was dedicated to Amaterasu Omikami, the Sun Goddess from whom—according to Shinto mythology—the emperors of Japan were descended.

Above An Edo period screen depicting Ariwara on his journey along the Narrow Ivy Road. It illustrates another of his autobiographical poems from the Tales of Ise. Each tale—not all of them by Ariwara—tells how some poems came to be written.

night stand," the way that the man left his lover's bedroom the following morning could make or break him. In the late 10th century, Sei Shonagon—a maid of honor to the emperor's daughter—recorded in her *Pillow Book* (the best surviving record of daily life in the capital):

> "Indeed a woman's attachment to a man depends largely on the elegance of his leave-taking. When he jumps out of bed, scurries about the room, lightly fastens his trouser-sash, rolls up the sleeves of his Court cloak, hunting costume or what-not, stuffs his belongings into the breast of his robe and then briskly secures the outer sash—she really begins to hate him."

But however well lovers followed the prescriptions of the polygamous world of Japanese aristocracy, such conduct carried with it unavoidable problems. Men were expected to keep second wives and have casual liaisons—if they did not, they were considered less impressive as husbands. Yet natural feelings of jealousy still existed. The love poem of Narihira and the imperial princess shows the refining touch given to a potentially problematic practice. They performed the ritual etiquette of love to perfection, and their exchange of verses gave a sense of permanence to what was in reality a chance and transient affair.

Pietro Bembo to *Lucrezia Borgia*

Above *The young Pietro Bembo, painted c. 1504 by Raphael, captures some of the aristocratic good looks that so attracted Lucrezia.*

Venice
October 18, 1503

Eight days have passed since I parted from f. f., and already it is as though I had been eight years away from her, although I can avow that not one hour has passed without her memory which has become such a close companion to my thoughts that now more than ever is it the food and sustenance of my soul; and if it should endure like this a few days more, as seems it must, I truly believe it will in every way have assumed the office of my soul, and I shall then live and thrive on the memory of her as do other men upon their souls, and I shall have no life but in this single thought. Let the God who so decrees do as he will, so long as in exchange I may have as much a part of her as shall suffice to prove the gospel of our affinity is founded on true prophecy. Often I find myself recalling, and with what ease, certain words spoken to me, some on the balcony with the moon as witness, others at that window I shall always look upon so gladly, with all the many endearing and gracious acts I have seen my gentle lady perform—for all are dancing about my heart with a tenderness so wondrous that they inflame me with a strong desire to beg her to test the quality of my love. For I shall never rest content until I am certain she knows what she is able to enact in me and how great and strong is the fire that her great worth has kindled in my breast. The flame of true love is a mighty force, and most of all when two equally matched wills in two exalted minds contend to see which loves the most, each striving to give yet more vital proof....It would be the greatest delight for me to see just two lines in f.f.'s hand, yet I dare not ask so much. May your Ladyship beseech her to perform whatever you feel is best for me. With my heart I kiss your Ladyship's hand, since I cannot with my lips.

On October 15, 1502, Pietro Bembo, a 32-year-old Venetian poet and one of the most accomplished scholars in Renaissance Italy, came to stay in Ostellato, a village close to the city-state of Ferrara in northern Italy. He was visiting his friend, the poet Ercole Strozzi at the Strozzi family villa. Soon after he arrived, another of the poet's friends, the beautiful and cultured Lucrezia Borgia visited the villa, and the two were instantly attracted.

Lucrezia, wife of Alfonso d'Este, who was heir to the dukedom of Ferrara, was daughter of Pope Alexander VI, of whom Machiavelli wrote,

"[he] never thought of anything but deceiving people."
Although she was barely 23, Lucrezia had already played a significant part in the intrigues of the Borgia family, and had been given in marriage three times to cement political alliances. Her father arranged a divorce from her first husband, Don Gasparo de Procida, and cancelled her betrothal to Ludovico Sforza, the powerful ruler of Milan. In 1500 her brother Cesare Borgia was suspected by many of having arranged the murder of her second husband, Alfonso, prince of Salerno. When she became first lady of Ferrara in 1502, Lucrezia acquired more wealth and a higher social position than ever before. She also had a good deal of freedom. Alfonso pursued his interests in military equipment, and left his wife to follow her own enthusiasms—poetry, music, and dancing. She became a prominent patron of the arts, attracting the flattery of poets and scholars from all over Italy.

Below In the summer of 1503 Bembo received this long lock of golden hair from Lucrezia as a token of her love. He carried it around with him, wrapped inside a folded sheet of vellum, and secured by ribbons. Today it is in the Ambrosian Library, Milan.

Above The Este castle in Ferrara, Lucrezia's family home where her third husband, Alfonso d'Este, had his court. It was here that Lucrezia began her secret correspondence with the handsome Venetian poet, Pietro Bembo.

This was the circle that Bembo joined in 1502. Tall, blond, and handsome, he was a master of courtly manners and a famous writer. He brought with him to Ostellato an unfinished book, *Gl'Asoliani*, a dialogue on the nature of love. In addition to these accomplishments, he had perfected the art of writing well-crafted and memorable love letters. Talking with Lucrezia, the conversation turned naturally to the subject of courtly love. Pietro's letter, extracted here, recalls their conversations,

"on the balcony with the moon as witness."
In 16th-century Italy, a man of letters and a lady of rank were almost expected to talk and write to each other at a level suspended somewhere between poetry and courtship. Two hundred years before, Francesco Petrarch (1304–74) wrote passionate poems to a woman called Laura, whom he saw only once, in church, and probably never spoke to. This set a powerful precedent. Every lady at a Renaissance court became a potential Laura, whom it was a poet's duty to praise from a distance. This ideal of pure and expressive love—always desiring and

never satisfied—was delicately, perhaps impossibly balanced. By June 1503 Lucrezia and Bembo were writing regularly, exchanging poems and endearments. Lucrezia cloaked her identity under the initials f. f. and as added concealment, Pietro sent his letters as if to one of her ladies-in-waiting. They made the relationship an elaborate game, played at arm's length and conducted through expressive letters rather than physical contact. Receiving a lock of her hair in the middle of that summer, Pietro expressed his joy:

> *"Every day you find some new way to fan my ardor."*

A few months later, in August 1503, Lucrezia's father died. She was grief stricken, refusing to eat and sitting all day in black-draped rooms. Apart from the emotional loss, he had been her chief protector from political maneuvering in her husband's court. Now the Borgia enemies had an opportunity for revenge. Bembo consoled Lucrezia, beset by dangers in an unfriendly court. He wrote,

> *"though it would be my greatest joy to see you happy in everything always, I affirm and I swear that rather than diminish my ardor, these misfortunes will quicken my desire to serve you."*

In October Bembo had to go back to Venice on family business. It was then that he wrote the letter extracted here. From December 1503 business kept him in Venice more or less permanently, but they continued to correspond. By early 1505 their letters were full of allusions to plots and intrigues threatening Lucrezia's position. Realizing that he could do little to protect her, Bembo wrote:

> *"the day will come when fate will overcome you in spite of our efforts to prevent it. But then it will be sweet to remember that our love was strong and constant, and the memory will make me happy."*

Right *A medal, thought to have been commissioned by Lucrezia before 1505 as a love token for Pietro. It features her portrait on one side and an image of Cupid on the other, with a secret inscription (see **below**) including the initials F. F., their code for Lucrezia.*

PIETRO BEMBO
(1470–1547)
was one of the most respected poets and scholars of his day. He was born into an aristocratic Venetian family, and had a brilliant career, achieving notable success in politics, the church, and the arts. His most important appointments were as secretary to Pope Leo X from 1513 to 1521, historiographer of Venice from 1529, and librarian of St. Mark's Cathedral beginning in approximately 1530. In 1539 he was made a cardinal, and for the remaining years of his life he devoted himself to theology and ancient history. In the field of the arts, he wrote a dialogue on love, *Gl'Asoliani*, dedicated to Lucrezia Borgia, and compiled one of the earliest Italian grammars. He also helped to establish Italian as a literary language, and was deeply involved in the development of the printing process.

LUCREZIA BORGIA
(1480–1519)
was the daughter of the Spanish cardinal, Rodrigo Borgia, later Pope Alexander VI, and his mistress Vannozza Catanei. The Borgias were notorious for their ruthless pursuit of power in Renaissance Italy, and Lucrezia has often been represented as one of the most grasping of the family. However, in retrospect it seems that she was the pawn of her scheming father and bloodthirsty brother, Cesare. The most unsavory rumors began in 1501, surrounding Lucrezia's 3-year-old son, Giovanni, who was recognized by two Papal bulls, first as the child of Alexander, and then as the child of Cesare. After the death of her father in 1503, Lucrezia led a calmer life with her third husband at the court of Ferrara, where she was a celebrated patron of the arts. In her 30's she became deeply religious. She died at age 39.

Chief among these dangers was the constant fear that Lucrezia's enemies might use Bembo to engineer a rift with her husband. Pietro cautioned her:

> *"...see that no one observes you writing for I know that you are watched."*

After this, apparently, they judged the correspondence to be too risky, and there were no more letters to f. f., only a few formal letters to the duchess of Ferrara. In September 1505 Bembo wrote congratulating the duchess on the birth of a son, and other conventional greetings passed between them in 1513 and 1514. They exchanged their last letters in 1517, two years before Lucrezia died; he expressed regret that he had not been able to see her on a recent visit to the region, and she echoed the sentiment. In fact, there is no evidence that they ever saw each other again.

Right *Lucrezia is believed to have been the model for St. Catherine in this detail from the painting* The Disputation of St. Catherine *by Pinturicchio, part of a fresco cycle that decorates the Vatican apartments once occupied by her father, Pope Alexander VI.*

Henry IV to Gabrielle d'Estrées

Above Henry IV of France and Navarre (c. 1596, painter unknown), dressed for battle and wearing the famous white cockade that he wore as he led his cavalry into battle.

From the battlefield before Dreux
June 16, 1593

I have waited patiently for one whole day without news of you; I have been counting the time and that's what it must be. But a second day—I can see no reason for it, unless my servants have grown lazy or been captured by the enemy, for I dare not put the blame on you, my beautiful angel: I am too confident of your affection—which is certainly due to me, for my love was never greater, nor my desire more urgent; that is why I repeat this refrain in all my letters: come, come, come, my dear love. Honor with your presence the man who, if only he were free, would go a thousand miles to throw himself at your feet and never move from there.

As for what is happening here, we have drained the water from the moat, but our cannon are not going to be in place until Friday when, God willing, I will dine in the town. The day after you reach Mantes, my sister will arrive at Anet, where I will have the pleasure of seeing you every day. I am sending you a bouquet of orange blossom that I have just received. I kiss the hands of the Vicomtesse [Gabrielle's sister, Françoise] if she is there, and of my good friend [his sister, Catherine of Bourbon], and as for you, my dear love, I kiss your feet a million times.

Above *The monogram Henry used in his early letters to Gabrielle.*

Henry IV, France's hero king of the late 16th century, is one of history's more surprising lovers. A commanding authority in state affairs, he saved and rebuilt a ruined country after the Wars of Religion in France, and also served as a figurehead for Catholic renewal. Yet he repeatedly allowed his heart to rule his head, threatening his political achievements in the process. No woman so affected him as the beautiful young Gabrielle d'Estrées, his lover for nine years, mother of three of his children, and his wife and queen in all but name. When heavily embroiled in military campaigns during the early years of their affair, Henry would lodge Gabrielle in a town at a safe distance from the fighting so that he could visit her from the battlefront. He sent her letters via servants almost daily, sometimes twice a day. The letter extracted is typical of his 35 surviving letters to her, many of which were not only amorous but also tinged with jealousy. At the time the letter was written she was a young beauty of 20, he a soldier of 40, married in a political alliance to the Catholic Marguerite de Valois, and known for his infidelities.

Henry first saw Gabrielle in November 1590 at her father's chateau in Coeuvres, Picardy, while civil war raged between the Catholic and Protestant forces. Contemporary accounts praise her long golden hair, her delicate rose complexion, and her exquisite figure. After his failure to take Paris from the militant Catholics of the Holy League in the fall of 1590, Henry's advisers counseled him to attack the city of Rouen, the League's greatest northern stronghold after Paris. But Henry, who by this time had designs on Gabrielle, instead lay siege to the less strategically important city of Chartres (February to April 1591), where Gabrielle's

Right *Henry's elegant handwriting closely covers a page from a letter he wrote to Gabrielle on October 29, 1598, praising her and their children.*

family had important interests, and restored her uncle as governor of the city. From that time on Gabrielle became his constant companion.

To keep Gabrielle from rival suitors, Henry married her off to an elderly widower, Nicolas d'Amerval, sieur of Liencourt, in June 1592. Throughout the following year, he sent her letter after passionate letter, jealousy sometimes getting the better of him. On April 15, for example, he wrote:

> "My beautiful love, you are indeed to be admired, yet why should I praise you? Up to now, aware of my passion, triumph has made you unfaithful…"

But five days later he had forgotten his jealousy and wanted only to be with her again:

> "Tomorrow I shall kiss your beautiful hands a thousand times. I can already feel the relief from my troubles that that hour will bring, which I hold as dear as my life; but if you delay by even one day, I shall die….To pass the month of April without one's mistress is not to live."

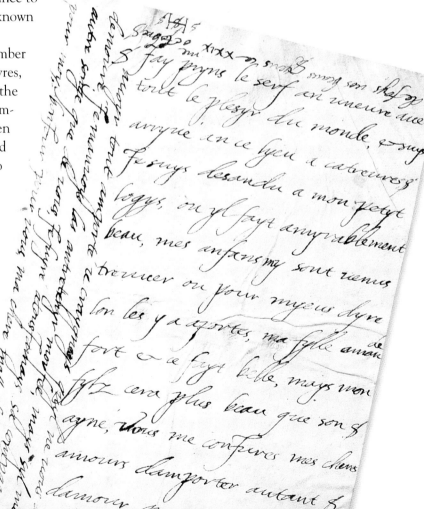

Whether Gabrielle was motivated more by love or ambition, she certainly put herself in some danger by accompanying him on his campaigns. In her one surviving letter to him, probably written sometime in February 1593, she wrote:

> *"Believe me, I am dying of fright. I beg you to let me know how things are with the most wonderful man in the world. I fear that your troubles must be great, for no other reason would deprive me of your presence today…"*

In June Henry wrote the letter extracted here, full of anticipation at their next meeting; by autumn, Gabrielle was pregnant with their first child.

Meanwhile, in July 1593 Henry converted to Catholicism to consolidate his hold on the crown, a step many considered to be a cynical act of statesmanship. But in a letter to Gabrielle he suggested it was not something he did lightly, as he wrote,

> *"tomorrow I shall make a perilous leap…"*

He closed the letter,

> *"…come early tomorrow, my love; it seems already as if a year has passed since I last saw you. I kiss a million times the beautiful hands of my angel and the mouth of my dear mistress."*

On February 27, 1594, Henry's coronation took place in Chartres cathedral. In June Gabrielle gave birth to their son, César. The following September she and Henry entered Paris together, with a magnificent escort, in public recognition of her status as the king's unofficial consort.

France, however, was still in a dangerous state of turmoil. In January 1595 Henry formally declared war on Spain. A year of fighting drained the country's finances, and by the winter Henry was very short of money. Gabrielle could have remained in luxury with César in Paris. She chose instead to join Henry for Christmas at the chateau of Folembray, only eight miles from the town of La Fère, which Henry was besieging. He was able to take the town the following spring only because Gabrielle gave up her diamonds as security for a loan from the grand duke of Tuscany. A contemporary historian wrote the following observation:

> *"This lady knew how to keep the affections of that great prince, so that he was as faithful to her as she was to him, for he looked at no other woman and it would be difficult to say which of the two was the fonder."*

By the end of 1596 it was clear that Henry wanted to marry Gabrielle and make César his official heir. He had her marriage to Liencourt annulled, and gave

Below *The palace of Fontainebleau, set amid hunting forests, was one of Henry's favorite residences. He greatly enlarged the palace itself and also ordered the landscaping of the gardens.*

The Lovers

HENRY IV OF FRANCE
(1553–1610)
was the first Bourbon king of France. He brought a high degree of unity to a country riven by religious differences. King of Navarre from 1572 and king of France from 1589, he was a skilled negotiator and a brilliant soldier in the field. He vacillated between Catholicism and Protestantism a number of times, partly to aid his political policy at the time, and partly because he was genuinely tolerant of both. He married twice, first in 1572 to his Catholic cousin Marguerite de Valois and again in 1600 to Marie de Médicis. But Gabrielle d'Estrées was probably the woman who exerted the most influence on him. He fathered her three children, along with many others by other mistresses and his second wife. He was assassinated in Paris in 1610.

GABRIELLE D'ESTRÉES
(1573–99),
daughter of the marquis of Coeuvres, became mistress to Henry IV in 1591, at age 18, and remained so until her death in childbirth at the age of 26. Her family was manipulative and power seeking, and there is much dispute as to whether Gabrielle was used by them or self-seeking in her unsuccessful pursuit of the title Queen of France. Henry certainly regarded her as his wife in all but name. She had three children by him, César, Catherine-Henriette, and Alexandre, all of whom were legitimized, founding the Vendôme branch of the House of Bourbon.

Above "La belle Gabrielle" in her bath (a painting of the mid-16th century; French School). Widely praised by contemporary observers for her great beauty, she was just 17 years old when she captivated the king with her charms and became his mistress.

her a string of titles. But before she could become queen, he had to obtain an annulment of his own marriage to Marguerite de Valois. Such a step could easily have led to a war of succession after his death and destroyed all his hard-won political achievements. To show how serious his intentions were, he gave Gabrielle the great diamond ring that had symbolized his marriage to France at his coronation.

During Holy Week 1599, fate took a hand. Henry was at Fontainebleau, while Gabrielle, expecting their third child, was in Paris. She went into a difficult labor on Maundy Thursday, and died in childbirth the next day, in such agony that she was rumored to have been poisoned. A mourning Henry wrote:

"the roots of love are dead within me and will never spring to life again."

John Wilmot, Earl of Rochester to Elizabeth Barry

1675

Madam,

So much wit and beauty as you have should think of nothing less than doing miracles, and there cannot be a greater than to continue to love me. Affecting everything is mean, as loving pleasure and being fond where you find merit; but to pick out the wildest and most fantastical odd man alive, and to place your kindness there, is an act so brave and daring as will show the greatness of your spirit and distinguish you in love, as you are in all things else, from womankind. Whether I have made a good argument for myself I leave you to judge, and beg you to believe me whenever I tell you what Mrs. B. is, since I give you so sincere an account of her humblest servant. Remember the hour of a strict account, when both hearts are to be open and we obliged to speak freely, as you ordered it yesterday (for so I must ever call the day I saw you last, since all time between that and the next visit is no part of my life, or at least like a long fit of the falling sickness wherein I am dead to all joy and happiness). Here's a damned impertinent fool bolted in that hinders me from ending my letter. The plague of **** take him and any man or woman alive that take my thoughts off of you. But in the evening I will see you and be happy, in spite of all the fools in the world.

Your humble servant
Rochester

Right *An oil painting of Elizabeth Barry, completed c. 1700, in the style of the leading portrait painter of the day, Godfrey Kneller.*

The story of John Wilmot, earl of Rochester, and the actress Elizabeth Barry has similarities to the famous play *Pygmalion* by George Bernard Shaw (adapted in 1956 by the lyricist Alan Lerner and the composer Frederick Loewe into the famous musical *My Fair Lady*). It started with a bet made in 1674. The love story that followed was outrageous and touching. Rochester wrote the letter extracted here in 1675 with characteristic humor, originality, and solemnity, echoing the language of the Anglican communion service in the phrase,

"when both hearts are to be open."

Rochester, poet at the court of England's Charles II, was as quoted here,

"the wildest and most fantastical odd man alive."

He also had an irrepressible eye for the women, including the beautiful heiress, Elizabeth Malet.

Seven years before his romance with Barry, the 18-year-old Rochester abducted the heiress, Malet, snatching her from a coach from under the nose of her aged guardian, Lord Hawley. Rochester was pursued, arrested, and briefly imprisoned in the Tower of London, before begging and receiving the king's forgiveness. Shortly after her rescue, Elizabeth rejected other more wealthy suitors and unexpectedly married Rochester on January 29, 1667. During the years that followed, the young earl lived a double life: at Adderbury, his country house in Oxfordshire, he enjoyed the forgiveness of his wife; at court he pursued a freewheeling, scandalous life.

Elizabeth Barry was not an obvious choice for Rochester. Her stage début in 1675 was distinctly unimpressive, and according to contemporary opinion she was in fact quite ugly. One wit wrote of her that she was,

"The finest woman in the world upon the stage and the ugliest woman oft on't."

In spite of these seeming disadvantages, Rochester made a bet with friends that he could make her into a successful actress in six months.

TO THE

Right Honourable

JOHN,

Earl of Rochefter,

One of the Gentlemen of His MAJESTY's Bed-Chamber, &c.

MY LORD,

Dedications are grown Things of so nice a Nature, that it is almoft impoffible for me to pay your Lordfhip thofe Acknowments I owe you, and not (from thofe who can not judge of the Sentiments I have of your Lordfhip's Favours) incurr the Cenfure either of a Fawner or a Flatterer. Both which ought to be as hateful to an Ingenious Spirit as Ingratitude. None of thefe would I be guilty of, and yet in letting the World know how Good and how Generous a Patron

A 2

Perfons Reprefented in the FARCE.

			By	Mr. Sandford. Mr. Noakes.
Thrifty, Gripe,	}	Two old Merchants,		Mr. Norris. Mr. Percivall.
Octavian, Leander,	}	Their Sons,		Mr. Anth. Leigh.
Scapin, a Cheat				Mr. Richards. Mr.——
Shift, Sly,	}	Scapin's Inftruments,		
Lucia, Thrifty's Daughter, Clara, Gripe's Daughter,				Mrs. Barry. Mrs. Gibbs.

The SCENE DOVER.

TITUS

Above *Thomas Otway's play* Titus and Berenice, *published in 1677, was dedicated to the playwright's patron, John, Earl of Rochester, "one of the gentlemen of His Majesty's Bed-Chamber." The original cast list shows that Elizabeth Barry played the role of Lucia in the farce scene.*

Left *The Duke's Theatre, Dorset Garden, London, where Elizabeth performed in many plays. It was designed in the baroque style by the English architect Christopher Wren and opened in 1671.*

She apparently had a good voice, and Rochester put her through intensive training that taught her to understand and interpret the feelings of the characters she played. He won his bet; Elizabeth was very successfully launched on the road to both wealth and fame. For the two years that their love affair lasted, Rochester, who was genuinely infatuated with his mistress—some contemporaries said that she was the love of his life—wrote her many adoring letters, of which the following extract is typical:

"...seeing you is as necessary to my life as breathing, so that I must see you or be yours no more, for that's the image I have of dying."

Winning the bet, however, carried its own risk: the loss of exclusivity. The theater was a place of low morality, and Elizabeth Barry's prominence meant that she received the advances of many other men. Reveling in her popularity, she swiftly developed a reputation as a

"mercenary prostituting dame."

An untitled lyric, written in his own handwriting in 1676 or 1677, was probably addressed to Elizabeth:

"Leave this gaudy gilded stage
From custom more than use frequented,
Where fools of either sex and age
Crowd to see themselves presented."

In 1677 Elizabeth gave birth to his child, a daughter whom they also called Elizabeth. The affair ended soon after this, and the following year, for reasons not known, Rochester took his baby daughter out of Barry's care. He also remembered her in his will. After their separation, Elizabeth Barry's fame made it possible for her to pursue an independent life, and her one-time sponsor seemed reconciled:

"...'tis impossible for me to curse you, but give me leave to pity myself, which is more than ever you will do for me."

Rochester returned to his family, and they spent a peaceful few years together, away from the court after his many years of over-indulgence. In the end husband and wife died within a year of each other.

During his last months, with his health in decline, Rochester turned his thoughts to serious matters. He developed an interest in philosophy and religion, discussing both with his friend Gilbert Burnet, royal chaplain and later Bishop of Salisbury. Rochester, at age 33, was a physical wreck. He had, in the words of the famous 18th-century critic Dr. Samuel Johnson,

❧ The Lovers ❧

JOHN WILMOT, EARL OF ROCHESTER
(1647–80)
was born in Ditchley, Oxfordshire, the son of a Puritan mother and a Royalist father. After the Restoration of Charles II in 1660, Rochester was rewarded with a royal pension of £500 a year for his father's loyalty to Charles I. From 1662 to 1664 he traveled on the Continent with his tutor, the Scottish physician Sir Andrew Balfour. In 1665, after a failed attempt to abduct the heiress, Elizabeth Malet, he was appointed a commander in the navy and distinguished himself in battle. In 1667 he married Elizabeth Malet and began to write a series of love lyrics, ostensibly addressed to her. Within a few years Rochester's reckless personality involved him in a series of escapades. Though his poetry and satires were much admired and he became a leading literary figure, he gradually sank into illness and depression. On his deathbed he experienced a religious conversion and repented his lifelong excesses.

ELIZABETH BARRY
(1658–1713)
was brought up by Sir William Davenant, a friend of the earl of Rochester. When she first met the young earl in 1675 she had just started her acting career. To win a bet, Rochester undertook her training for the stage and promoted her in fashionable society, in return for which she became his mistress from 1675 to 1677. Her first success was as Leonora in Aphra Behn's *Abdelazar* (July 1676), after which she played a number of leading roles including Hellena in Aphra Behn's *The Rover*, Emillia in D'Urfey's *A Fond Husband*, and Philisides in *The Constant Nymph*. In December 1677 she bore Rochester a daughter, Elizabeth Clarke, whom he took out of her care, possibly in the summer of 1678, and who died when she was 12 or 13 years old. Elizabeth Barry went on to have a prolonged and brilliant career, establishing her reputation as England's leading actress in her performance of Monimia in Otway's *The Orphan*. She died at age 55.

"Blazed out his youth and health in lavish voluptuousness."

At the end, however, Rochester made an unexpected conversion to religion under the guidance of Burnet, who stayed at his bedside. He had lived a life ruled by the emotions: passion, jealousy, devotion, and forgiveness. After he died, his contemporary, the playwright Aphra Behn, wrote of him:

"He was but lent this duller World t'improve
In all the charms of Poetry and Love;
Both were his gift, which freely he bestow'd,
And like a God, dealt to the wond'ring Crowd."

Elizabeth Barry outlived Rochester by 33 years and became the most celebrated actress of the day.

Right *Lord Rochester and his monkey, from an oil painting attributed to Jacob Huysmans, and completed c.1665–70, when the earl was a naval commander in his early twenties. He served with distinction in the war against the Dutch (1665–67).*

Johann von Goethe to Charlotte von Stein

June 17, 1784

My letters will have shown you how lonely I am. I don't dine at Court, I see few people, and take my walks alone, and at every beautiful spot I wish you were there. I can't help loving you more than is good for me; I shall feel all the happier when I see you again.

I am always conscious of my nearness to you, your presence never leaves me. In you I have a measure for every woman, for everyone; in your love a measure for all that is to be. Not in the sense that the rest of the world seems obscure to me, on the contrary, your love makes it clear; I see quite clearly what men are like and what they plan, wish, do and enjoy; I don't grudge them what they have, and comparing is a secret joy to me, possessing as I do such an imperishable treasure.

You in your household must feel as I often do in my affairs; we often don't notice objects simply because we don't choose to look at them, but things acquire an interest as soon as we see clearly the way they are related to each other. For we always like to join in, and the good man takes pleasure in arranging, putting in order and furthering the right and its peaceful rule.

The elephant's skull is coming with me to Weimar.

My rock studies are going very well.

Fritz is happy and good. Without noticing it, he is taken into the world, and so without knowing it, he will become familiar with it. It is still all a game to him; yesterday I got him to read some petitions and give me summaries of them; he laughed like anything and wouldn't believe that people could be in such straits as these petitions made out.

Adieu, you whom I love a thousand times.

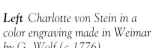

Left *Charlotte von Stein in a color engraving made in Weimar by G. Wolf (c.1776).*

The German playwright, poet, novelist, intellectual, Johann Wolfgang von Goethe, met Charlotte von Stein in November 1775. At the age of 33, she was seven years his senior, wife of the duke of Weimar's master-of-horse, and the mother of seven children. She nevertheless responded warmly to Goethe, who was invited to the Weimar court by the duke, Karl August, with whom he became very close friends. For Charlotte von Stein, Goethe's intellectual conversation and broad interests brought a breath of fresh air to provincial Weimar, which was scarcely more than a village surrounding the ducal residence. Goethe in turn fell deeply in love with Charlotte. They began an "affair" that was, for the most part, a true marriage of minds. Ten years after they met, as the letter extracted here illustrates, their relationship was still as intense as when it began. This letter is just one of more than 1,500 letters and notes that Charlotte received from him.

Before Goethe met Charlotte, he was shown a portrait of her, and wrote in response:

> "It would be a magnificent spectacle to see how the world is reflected in this soul. She sees the world as it is, and yet through the medium of love. And mildness is the predominant impression."

When they met, he found "mildness" one of her most attractive qualities. In his verses, in which he referred to her as "Lida," he wrote of the peace and serenity she brought him. They apparently shared more than this. As Goethe wrote:

> "We first know we exist when we recognize ourselves in others."

Right *Goethe and Charlotte's son, Fritz, his pupil from 1783, in a contemporary silhouette (artist unknown). Not believing in formal education, Goethe chose to bring up Fritz himself.*

Above *A miniature of Goethe painted in 1779 by Johann Heinrich Wilhelm Tischbein, and (right) a letter Goethe wrote to Charlotte in 1782, at the height of his passion for her.*

Charlotte kept the relationship firmly within the bounds permitted by late 18th-century German society. With her husband away from home, often for days at a time, Goethe was her devoted attendant. She, in turn, was his idealized love. In a letter he wrote her in September 1776—the year after they met—he clearly expressed the strain he felt at having to maintain a socially acceptable distance from her, as decorum required:

> "Why should I torture you, dearest creature? Why deceive myself and plague you? We cannot be anything to each other, and we are too much to each other…"

After six years of a steadily deepening friendship, Goethe wrote a letter on March 12, 1781, which suggests a turning point in their relationship, and points to liaisons having taken place:

> "My soul has grown fast to yours…. I am inseparable from you, and…neither height nor depth can keep me from you. I wish there were some sort of vow or sacrament that would make me yours, visibly or legally. And my period of probation was long enough to think it all over."

As described in the letter written three years later, extracted here, their relationship continued unresolved. Goethe became tutor to Charlotte's son, Fritz, in 1783, which gave him further contact with her. He found consolation in the idealized image of Charlotte, present to him even when she was not there. Yet he declared himself lonely.

From about 1780 on, his creative spirit seems to have dimmed, perhaps because he felt stifled by his emotional dependence on Charlotte. His poetry from this period is more pedantic, and though he wrote a few plays for the entertainment of the court, most of his time was devoted to official duties and the scientific study of anatomy, botany, and geology. By 1785, he blamed Weimar, and perhaps Charlotte, for his unfulfilled hopes:

"*I cannot and will not bury my talents,*"
he wrote.

The following year, while vacationing in Karlsbad, Bohemia, Goethe suddenly left for Italy, incognito. He stayed for nearly two years, steeping himself in classical culture, as well as in the country's atmosphere and warmth. In letters home—he wrote to Charlotte nearly every day—he said he felt reborn:

"*Though still the same as ever, I feel transformed to the innermost marrow.*"

He returned to Weimar in 1788. Charlotte—instead of being joyful—reproached him for having been away.

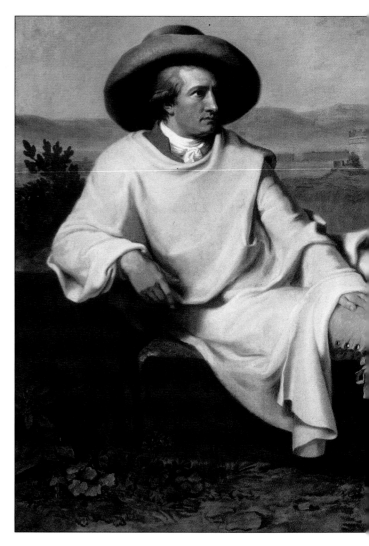

Left *Goethe's garden house, in the grounds of Weimar park. He would retreat to the peace and quiet of this cottage—shaded by trees that he planted himself—to study and write his books and papers.*

Below *Goethe's writing implements, which he used to write countless letters to his muse and inspiration, Charlotte von Stein.*

JOHANN WOLFGANG VON GOETHE
(1749–1832)
is regarded by many as a German literary genius. Brought up in Frankfurt-am-Main, he studied law in Leipzig and Strassburg. In 1774 he wrote the popular *Die Leiden des jungen Werthers (The Sorrows of Young Werther)*, which caused a sensation. From 1775 on he lived in Weimar, where he met and fell in love with Charlotte von Stein, inspiration for the heroine of his play *Iphigenie auf Tauris* (1787) and Natalie in his *Wilhelm Meister* novels. He spent two years (1786–88) in Italy, then returned to Weimar. In 1808 he produced the first part of his most famous work, *Faust* (1808; part II, 1832). He also wrote works on botany and biology, an autobiography, *Dichtung und Wahrheit*, and a collection of verses, *West-Östlicher Divan* (1819), among many other writings. In addition, his official duties at the Weimar court included director of the war department, adviser to the duke, and director of mines and all scientific and artistic institutions, including the theater.

CHARLOTTE VON STEIN
(NÉE VON SCHARDT)
(1742–1827)
was the eldest daughter of Weimar's master of court ceremonies. In 1758 she became lady-in-waiting to the duchess, Anna Amalia, and in 1764 married Friedrich, Freiherr von Stein, equerry to Duke Karl August. In 1775—the mother of seven children— she met Goethe. The following year she began an intimate friendship with him that lasted some 13 years. An accomplished singer and artist, she was also well read, and in 1776 wrote a humorous piece, *Rino*, on Goethe and the women of the court. Their friendship ended after Goethe's two- year visit to Italy without her. Four years later, in 1792, she wrote a prose tragedy, *Dido* (published 1867), which contains many references to her break with him.

Above Goethe in the Campagna, *painted by J. H. W. Tischbein in 1787 during Goethe's two-year stay in Italy, a visit that profoundly changed his thinking, and had a major impact on his relationship with Charlotte.*

Despite all the letters he had written to her from Italy, she felt excluded from the experience that had produced such an effect on him. In response to her reproaches, Goethe wrote:

"If you could but listen to me, I would gladly tell you, that although your reproaches pain me at the moment, they leave no trace of anger in my heart against you."

In response to another letter from her shortly afterward he wrote:

"And it must be by a miracle indeed if I should have forgotten the best, the deepest relation of all, that, namely, to thee....But I freely confess that the manner in which you have treated me hitherto is not to be endured..."

That year Goethe met a young woman, Christiane Vulpius, who became his mistress. For 13 years Charlotte had been his Romantic ideal, a kindred spirit and a muse. But she could not forgive him. She rejected his offers of friendship, and ridiculed him in public. Christiane, by contrast, was loving and affectionate. She remained loyal to Goethe for 18 years— and bore him several children—before they finally got married in 1806. Charlotte, some 13 years after the rift with Goethe, confessed her continued love for him in a letter to her son on January 12:

"I did not know that our former friend Goethe was still so dear to me that a severe illness from which he has been suffering for nine days, would so deeply affect me....I have shed many tears over him in the last few days; I deeply regret now that when he wished to visit me on New Year's Day, I, alas! because I lay ill with headache, excused myself, and now I shall perhaps never see him again."

George Bernard Shaw
to Ellen Terry

*The midnight train—gets to Dorking
at 1 (a.m.) 14th–15th June 1897—
stopping just now, but will joggle like mad presently*

*Do you read these jogged scrawls, I wonder. I think
of your poor eyes, and resolve to tear what I have
written up: then I look out at the ghostly country and
the beautiful night, and I cannot bring myself to read
a miserable book....Yes, as you guess, Ellen, I am
having a bad attack of you just at present. I am
restless; and a man's restlessness always means a
woman; and my restlessness means Ellen. And your
conduct is often shocking. Today I was wandering
somewhere…when I glanced at a shop window; and
there you were—oh disgraceful and abandoned—in
your third Act Sans Gene dress—a mere
waistband—laughing wickedly, and saying
maliciously: "Look here restless one, at your pillow, at
what you are really thinking about." How can you
look Window and Grove's camera in the face with such thoughts in your head and almost
nothing on....*

Above Ellen Terry as Madame Sans Gene in 1897, part of the publicity for the production of Sans Gene in the Lyceum Theatre, London.

*Oh fie, fie, let me get away from this stuff, which you have been listening to all your
life, & despise—though indeed, dearest Ellen, these silly longings stir up great waves of
tenderness in which there is no guile.*

*I shall find a letter from you when I get back to Lotus, shall I not? Reigate we are at
now; and it's a quarter to one. In ten minutes, Dorking station; in seventeen minutes
thereafter, Lotus, and a letter. Only a letter, perhaps not even that. O Ellen, what will you
say when the Recording Angel asks you why none of your sins have my name to them?*

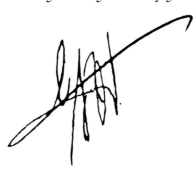

In the summer of 1892 the vivacious and beautiful British actress Ellen Terry exchanged a few letters with George Bernard Shaw, then a witty music critic. At first they wrote about an Italian soprano, a protégé of Ellen Terry, then they ranged over more personal topics. Shaw was 36 and had not yet made his name; Terry, at 45, was an international star. Shaw's letters moved quickly from being, as Ellen described them, "stiff and prim," to cosy intimate exchanges that delighted both of them. After a while, Shaw stopped writing, but not before he had made the declaration that Ellen Terry had

> "all the nameless charm, all the skill, all the force, in a word, all the genius"

needed to play Ibsen, the Norwegian dramatist who represented the new theater in the 1890's. He thought that as Sir Henry Irving's leading lady she was wasting herself in inept productions played in an outdated, though fashionable, theatrical style. In spite of all that, Shaw said, she had created her own

> "incomparable self...irresistible Ellen."

Three years later, in March 1895, Ellen Terry revived the correspondence. By this time Shaw was a controversial dramatist himself, interested in writing plays with strong parts for women. The state of the theater became a central theme in their intimate exchanges. It was, as Shaw described it,

> "a paper courtship...perhaps the pleasantest and most enduring of all courtships."

Shaw and Terry carefully avoided meeting, though they only lived 20 minutes apart. Instinct told them that meeting might spoil their open, playful delight in each other. Shaw, of course, saw Ellen on the stage, and her likeness often appeared in the newspapers and in shop windows. In one of her letters to Shaw, Ellen interrogated a photograph of him in an attempt to get closer to the real man:

> "So this is you, is it G.B.S? Well turn your eyes round to me, and don't hide your mouth (for that tells all about one!)...Is that your ear? I don't like it. It's rather like mine, but so much the worse for both of us. A lovely forehead...And your eyes? Look at me! Nicely cut nose, a jolly chin...And you are red! So am I, now..."

Her tone is a subtle mix of bold actress and coy lover—or perhaps even of a fond mother—musing on a photograph. There was a good deal of the maternal in Ellen's attitude to Shaw. He, for his part, clearly enjoyed being amorous in his letters. In October 1896, he wrote to Ellen:

> "Everything real in life is based on need: just so far as you need me I have you tightly in my arms; beyond that I am only a luxury..."

and then went on to describe his "love affairs." Ellen, whose experience of men was more thorough than Shaw's of women, responded with a simpler honesty:

Above George Bernard Shaw in the mid-1890's, when the success of his comic play Arms and the Man brought him his first taste of prosperity and literary recognition.

"I'll wait until you 'need' me, and then I'll mother you. That's the only unselfish love. I've never been admired or loved (properly) but one-and-a-half times in my life, and I am perfectly sick of loving. All on one side isn't fair."

The letters from this period suggest that neither one felt sure of where they stood.

The correspondence reached its peak in 1897—the year of the letter abridged here—when they were writing approximately every three days to each other. In another letter about that time Shaw wrote:

"Lord, what a supernal night it was last night in the train and coming home. A ten inch moon, a lime-light sky, nightingales, everything wonderful. Today, the same clearness and an Italian heat....I finished the revision of 'Mrs Warren' yesterday. And now I __must__ do some work. But—to sustain me in it—keep on loving me (if you ever did) my Ellenest—love me hard, love me soft, and deep, and sweet, and for ever and ever and ever."

A year later the affection remained, but the letters contained more talk of the theater. Perhaps Shaw was distracted by the green-eyed Irish millionairess, Charlotte Payne-Townshend, whom he met in 1896 and often talked about in his letters to Ellen. On June 1, 1898, Shaw and Charlotte were married. Ellen wrote, apparently without jealousy,

"How splendid! What intrepidity to make such a courageous bid for happiness. Into it you both go! Eyes wide open! An example to the world, and may all the gods have you in their keeping."

However, in the months that followed, the,

"perfect fury for writing letters to each other,"

as Ellen called it, slackened, and the content of their letters focused on new plays and theater gossip. In 1902 Shaw invited her to play Lady Cecily in *Captain Brassbound's Conversion*, a part he wrote with Ellen in mind. In her autobiography, she suggested that her letters must have been "good copy" because Lady Cecily's character came entirely from them. Ellen declined the part, but met Shaw for the first time at the opening of the production.

"He was quite unlike what I had imagined from his letters,"

she said enigmatically. In 1906 she finally played Lady Cecily on stage and found Shaw,

"wonderfully patient at rehearsals...a good, kind, gentle creature."

VEDRENNE-BARKER PERFORMANCES.

J. Vedrenne   *H. Granville Barker*

THIS EVENING, SATURDAY, APRIL 28th, 1906,

CAPTAIN BRASSBOUND'S CONVERSION

By *G. Bernard Shaw*

LADY CECILY WAYNFLETE ...	*Ellen Terry* ✱
SIR HOWARD HALLAM	*J. H. Barnes*
CAPTAIN BRASSBOUND ...	*Frederick Kerr*
REV. LESLIE RANKIN ...	*F. Cremlin*
FELIX DRINKWATER	*Edmund Gwenn*
REDBROOK	*C. Lillford Delph.*
JOHNSON	*Edmund Gurney.*
MARZO	*Michael Sherbrooke*
SIDI EL ASSIF	*Lewis Casson*
THE CADI OF KINTAFI ...	*Trevor Lowe.*
OSMAN	*Gordon-Bailey.*—
HASSAN	*Jules Shaw*
CAPT. HAMLIN KEARNEY, U.S.N.	*James Carew* ✗
AMERICAN BLUE JACKET	*Frederick Lloyd.*

ACT I.   Mogador.   The Missionary's Garden.
ACT II.   Meskala.   In a Castle on the Hills.
ACT III.   Mogador.   In the Missionary's House.

❧ *The Lovers* ❧

GEORGE BERNARD SHAW
(1856–1950)
was born into an impoverished branch of the Irish landed gentry. In 1876 he came to London to work as a journalist and arts critic, struggled for some years, but eventually embarked on a literary career. His first novels, written in the 1880's, were all failures, but he gained fame in other areas: as a socialist pamphleteer, a critic, an orator, and a campaigning vegetarian. In the 1890's, inspired by Ibsen, he began to write modern comic drama, which was hugely successful. Over the following years, his plays—including *Arms and the Man* (1894), *Candida* (1897), and *John Bull's Other Island* (1904)—became internationally admired. He was awarded the Nobel Prize for Literature in 1925 following the publication of his most acclaimed play, *St. Joan*, in 1924. Shaw was 94 when he died, attributing longevity to his vegetarian lifestyle.

ELLEN TERRY
(1847–1928)
was the most celebrated actress of her generation. After several false starts and two broken marriages, she began, in 1878, a 24-year partnership with the actor Sir Henry Irving, as his leading lady. The couple became famous internationally for their Shakespearean productions, but their partnership on stage was never formalized in marriage. When Irving's affection for her began to fade, Ellen began the famous "paper courtship" with Shaw. After the correspondence petered out she married in 1907 for the third and last time. Her new husband was the American actor James Carew; he was some 30 years younger than Ellen and the marriage soon broke up. She continued her career on the stage, in films, and as a Shakespearean lecturer, and was made a Dame Grand Cross of the British Empire in the year Shaw became a Nobel Laureate.

Above A program for the 1906 production of Captain Brassbound's Conversion, *autographed by the cast. Shaw wrote the play with Ellen in mind, but at first she refused the part of Lady Cecily Waynflete. Later she warmed to the idea when she realized that the character was modeled on her.*

Far left Sketches of scenes from Shaw's most famous play, Pygmalion, starring Ellen's great rival in the theater, Mrs. Patrick Campbell. "Mrs. Pat" was also a rival for Shaw's affections, and Ellen's successor in another of his love affairs on paper.*

Below A selection of Shaw's letters to Ellen spanning their long correspondence, which lasted from 1892 until 1918.*

For one who had been such a close confidante, she summed him up rather curiously in 1908:

> *"It doesn't answer to take Bernard Shaw seriously. He is not a man of conviction."*

Shaw, for his part, commented on the whole correspondence when it was published in 1931, three years after Ellen's death:

> *"…a clever woman's most amusing toys are interesting men."*

The letter romance had its season. If Shaw and Ellen Terry grew more distant with time, they could at least enjoy the memory of an intimacy some never experience.

Theodore Roosevelt, Jr.
to his wife, Bunny

May 20, 1943

Dearest Bunny,

Do you know what this is—a wedding anniversary letter. I think it should arrive about on the right date. Do you remember that hot June day thirty-three years ago?—the church jammed—Father with a lovely waistcoat with small blue spots— the Rough Riders—the ushers in cutaways—the crowds in the street—your long white veil and tight little bodice—the reception at Aunt Harriet's—Uncle Ed—your mother with one of her extraordinary hats that stood straight up.

And do you remember what the world was then—little and cozy—a different order of things, wars considered on the basis of a Dick [Richard Harding] Davis novel, a sort of "As it was in the beginning" atmosphere over life. We've come a long way down a strange road since then. Nothing has happened as we imagined it would except our children. We never thought we'd roam the world. We never thought our occupations and interests would cover such a range. We never thought that our thirty-third anniversary would find us deep in our second war and me again at the front. Well, darling, we've lived up to the most important part of the ceremony, "In sickness and in health, for richer for poorer, till death do you part."

Much, much love.

T & d.

Above *Brig. Gen. Theodore Roosevelt Jr., enjoying a letter from home on the bumper of his personalized "Rough Rider" jeep in 1944, the year he died.*

The letter extracted here, written in 1943 by Brig. Gen. Theodore Roosevelt, Jr., to his wife Eleanor (nicknamed Bunny) is a fine example of a love letter written in time of war. In it, Roosevelt—who commanded American troops during the Tunisian campaign and was son of former U.S. President Theodore Roosevelt—conjured up a vivid verbal snapshot of their wedding, and gave a touching survey of the path their lives had taken. It is just one of the hundreds of thousands of letters to and from the armed forces in which love shines through as the greatest human consolation.

Theodore and Eleanor first met on a railroad platform in New Haven, Connecticut, in October 1908. He was 21; she just 19. Both were on their way to the same house party. In her memoirs, *Day Before Yesterday*, Bunny recalled:

> "I was not eager to meet the President's eldest son, whose name seemed always in the papers, as I thought he would be conceited and bumptious."

As the eldest son of a U. S. president, young Roosevelt struggled to escape the shadow of his famous father. As Bunny wrote in her memoirs:

> "He was always accused of imitating his father in speech, walk and smile."

However, they found themselves seated next to each other at dinner. Bunny recalled how she was,

> "surprised and charmed to find him so agreeable."

He was a good listener, too, since, she continued,

> "even at that age he was keenly interested in people and in different points of view and had a remarkable faculty of making one feel at one's best."

Two years later, on June 20, 1910, they were married in New York. At the church 500 seats in the gallery were reserved for the Rough Riders—members of a cavalry regiment that Teddy senior had led into battle in Cuba during the Spanish-American War of 1898. (Ted junior referred to them in his letter

extracted here.) After the event, the newlyweds tried to avoid publicity, evading newsmen temporarily by registering at hotels under assumed names.

Bunny received valuable advice about marriage from a friend. In her memoirs she recounted some precepts she picked up, such as,

> "Don't be a yes-woman. Tell Ted frankly when you agree or disapprove....Never take him for granted. If you don't listen with sympathy and warmth whenever he tells you anything about himself, remember there are plenty of other women who will."

Ted was a businessman for many years. Yet in his letter of July 1921, he wrote,

> "I have decided to give you all my money. You have handled all our money affairs as far as spending is concerned ever since we were married. If I died, or if there was another war and I was lost, it would make it much simpler for you to have it all."

Left and above right *Ted's letter to Bunny on Victory ("V-Mail") stationary, designed to be put onto microfilm to speed delivery. In this way a ton of V-mail was reduced to just 25 lbs.*

Right *Eleanor's formal wedding portrait was taken a few days before her marriage to Ted on June 20, 1910. He recalled the event fondly in his 1943 wedding anniversary letter.*

Above *"Old Orchard," completed in 1938, was Theodore and Bunny's family home on Long Island, New York. Theodore lived here for only three years before returning to the army in 1941.*

❧ *The Lovers* ❧

THEODORE ROOSEVELT, JR., (1887–1944), the eldest child of U.S. President Theodore Roosevelt by his second wife, was born at Sagamore Hill, the family home in Oyster Bay, on New York's Long Island. In 1908 after attending Harvard, he went into business, and married Eleanor (Bunny) in 1910. In time they had four children. During World War I young Teddy fought in France and received many decorations for bravery. In the 1920's he entered politics, going on to hold several high offices, including assistant secretary of the Navy and governor of Puerto Rico. In 1941 he was made brigadier general and participated in the Tunisian and Italian campaigns of World War II. At the D-Day landings Roosevelt was the first infantry general to land (at Utah Beach); he was serving as military governor of Cherbourg when he died of a heart attack.

ELEANOR (BUNNY) BUTLER ALEXANDER ROOSEVELT (1889–1960) was the daughter of a prominent New York lawyer, Henry Addison, and Grace (Green) Alexander. She married Theodore Roosevelt, Jr., in 1910, and throughout her life not only supported him in his career, but also proved a highly organized, socially conscious person in her own right. She helped improve the conditions of Puerto Rican women while her husband was governor of the island (1929–31); she organized the first American women's committee for China Relief (1937); and she directed the American Red Cross Club in England (1942). Eleanor received citations and commendations from, among others, the French government, Gen. John J. Pershing, and the U.S. War Department. She also wrote a fascinating account of her life in her memoirs, *Day Before Yesterday*.

This was a trust unusual in their day, and of necessity, it extended to the upbringing of their children.

Bunny was not just a comfort to Ted when he was away. She also had an adventurous spirit. In the 1920's they went to Central Asia together. At the guarded Afghan frontier, they found a sign which forbade them to cross over. Bunny recalled saying to her husband,

> *"Someday let's come back and go all the way in."*

He replied jokingly,

> *"I'm taking no chances with you. We might do it when you're old and ugly."*

Ted and Bunny loved each other deeply, with a constancy born of maturity. Having survived the horrors of World War I, they were separated again for long periods during World War II. In 1942 Ted went first to England and then to North Africa in command of American troops. Eleanor, meanwhile, worked for the American Red Cross in England. Ted wrote often. In 1944 he wrote to her from England after attending their son Quentin's wedding,

> *"Thank God I was here at this time, but I miss you something awful."*

He did not have long to live. On June 5, 1944, the night before the Normandy D-Day landings, he wrote,

> *"We've had a grand life and I hope there'll be more…in our years together we've packed in enough for ten ordinary lives.… We have been very happy. I pray we may be together again."*

The last letter to Bunny was dated July 10, 1944. It told of the day's events, and included the simple but poignant statement,

> *"I'm glad you've liked my letters."*

Two days later he died of a heart attack, at age 56. A focus of public interest for most of their lives, Theodore and Eleanor had maintained a marriage of remarkable stability and closeness for 34 years. In his marriage to Bunny, Ted had found a sympathetic, loving soulmate who was able to share not only the good times but the hard times as well, and who understood his personal struggle to be judged on his own achievements—not those of his father. Theirs was a relationship of rare understanding.

Above This sampler—a decorative piece of needlework—was made by Eleanor for Theodore in 1934 as a souvenir of a hunting expedition that they went on together in Asia in the 1920's. In the center, a bearded Ted strides across a mountain range with rifle in hand. Ted advised Bunny on the correct markings of the animals he shot.

Right A Roosevelt family portrait, including dogs, shows (from left to right) Cornelius, Theodore junior, Eleanor (Bunny), Grace, Theodore III, with Quentin seated in front.

Passionate Love

". . . In our life there is a

single color,

as on an artist's palette,

which provides the

meaning of life and art.

It is the color of love."

MARC CHAGALL,
NEWSWEEK,
April 8, 1985

Napoleon to Josephine

Spring 1797

To Josephine,

I love you no longer; on the contrary, I detest you. You are a wretch, truly perverse, truly stupid, a real Cinderella. You never write to me at all, you do not love your husband; you know the pleasure that your letters give him yet you cannot even manage to write him half a dozen lines, dashed off in a moment!

What then do you do all day, Madame? What business is so vital that it robs you of the time to write to your faithful lover? What attachment can be stifling and pushing aside the love, the tender and constant love which you promised him? Who can this wonderful new lover be who takes up your every moment, rules your days and prevents you from devoting your attention to your husband? Beware, Josephine; one fine night the doors will be broken down and there I shall be.

In truth, I am worried, my love, to have no news from you; write me a four-page letter instantly made up from those delightful words which fill my heart with emotion and joy.

I hope to hold you in my arms before long, when I shall lavish upon you a million kisses, burning as the equatorial sun.

Bonaparte

Above *Napoleon picked sweet violets from Josephine's grave and wore them in a locket around his neck until his death seven years later.*

Right *Josephine's wedding ring given to her by Napoleon and inscribed with his initials and the words "Amour sincère," or sincere love.*

Right A detail from Napoleon on the Bridge of Arcole, by Gros, painted during the Italian campaign of 1796-97. The portrait was Josephine's idea, one of many occasions when Gros recorded a Napoleonic victory.

Left The empress Josephine, painted by Pierre Paul Prud'hon in 1805. Josephine was sketched and painted dozens of times during her life, and Napoleon always carried an image of her with him on his campaigns.

I n April 1795 a young Corsican artillery officer, Napoleon Bonaparte, was recalled to Paris from Marseilles on the French Mediterranean coast. He had distinguished himself in a number of battles fighting for the French Republic against British and French Royalist forces. Meanwhile, moderate republican politicians had been consolidating their hold on the country. In the capital the mood was buoyant. Writing to his brother Joseph on May 28, Napoleon described the whirlwind of activity going on in the city, noting just how much women had to do with the tone of Parisian life. It is, he wrote,

"the only place in the world where they deserve to steer the ship of state: the men are mad about them, think of nothing else, and live only for them…. Give a woman six months in Paris, and she knows where her empire is, and what is her due."

Just over four months later he fell passionately in love with Josephine. She was the widow of the aristocrat Alexandre de Beauharnais, a republican general guillotined in 1794 on the orders of Robespierre. Passion was the first step toward a complex and often troubled relationship, as the letter here shows.

Napoleon was called into service quickly and, on October 5, 1795, put down a Royalist mob attacking the Tuileries Palace. On October 9, the authorities ordered the surrender of all weapons in the districts of Paris most involved in the uprising. Eugène de Beauharnais, Josephine's 14-year-old son by her first marriage, went to the young Bonaparte, by now a general, to plead that they be allowed to keep his father's sword in memory of his service to the state. Touched by the boy's filial devotion, Napoleon granted the request. The next day Josephine, who had recently been mistress to Paul Barras, the most important man in the government, came to thank him. Napoleon—shrewdly calculating in war, but also a fiery romantic at heart—was beguiled by her grace and gentle charm. A bourgeois youth from Corsica, he fell in love with the widow of a member

of the old aristocracy, a class he claimed to despise.

Napoleon and Josephine soon became lovers, and on March 9, 1796, they were married at a civil wedding. Although Josephine was 33, six years older than Napoleon, they both gave their ages as 28. Two days later, Napoleon left Paris and Josephine to take command of the French army of Italy, seemingly forgotten in the Alps. Within a few months he transformed a band of demoralized men into one of the most potent military forces in Europe.

The daughter of an aristocrat planter, Josephine originally came from Martinique,

"an inhabitant of the isles of the ocean,"

as Napoleon called her. In 1779, at age 16, she left Martinique to marry de Beauharnais, son of a rich Orléans family. But she was too provincial for him, shallow and easily bored; in 1785 they separated.

It is not clear exactly what Josephine saw in the young Napoleon, described by one of France's leading politicians as,

"A little Corsican soldier of no account, who will give no trouble to anybody."

However, as a recently impoverished, pleasure-loving widow with two children to take care of—her only

Below *This magnificent casket, inscribed with the letter "J", was given to Josephine by Napoleon as a wedding present. The ceremony was on March 9, 1796.*

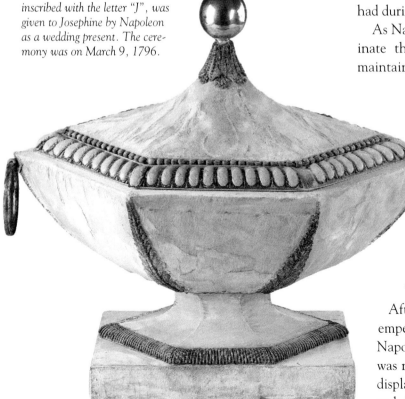

assets charm and a fragile beauty—she was surely eager for security. In addition, she was, at 33, getting on in years—15 was considered a marriageable age at the time—and she could not continue to depend on the generosity of her lovers.

If, for Josephine, the marriage meant protection and an entrée into Parisian society, for Napoleon it meant uncompromising passion. As he carried out his brilliant Italian campaign, he bombarded his new wife, Josephine, with a flood of emotional letters such as the one printed here. In a letter to his brother, Joseph, Napoleon wrote:

"I must see her and press her to my heart. I love her to the point of madness, and I cannot continue to be separated from her. If she no longer loved me, I would have nothing left to do on earth."

After his repeated pleadings, she followed him to Italy. During his Egyptian campaign of 1798–99, Napoleon heard that Josephine had for some time been conducting an affair with a handsome lieutenant, Hippolyte Charles. His initial anger softened (affairs were almost expected behavior at the time), and the two were reconciled. From this time onward, however, the relationship changed from extravagant passion on Napoleon's side to a mutual affection that survived the numerous affairs that Napoleon himself had during the course of their marriage.

As Napoleon conquered Europe and came to dominate the political scene in France, so Josephine maintained his houses and state palaces—and herself—at an appropriate level of splendor. She responded to her husband's whims—his love of makeup, for example, and his horror of perfume—and he paid her enormous bills for clothes, shoes, jewelry, and *objets d'art*. On state visits to cities throughout the nation she was always generous, kindly, and beguiling. As Napoleon himself once said,

"I only win battles; Josephine wins hearts for me."

After May 1804, when Napoleon was declared emperor, Josephine's position seemed secure. But Napoleon wanted an heir to rule after him. There was none. Josephine, increasingly fearful of being displaced as the empress, struggled against gossip and foreboding. She could be overwhelmed by

NAPOLEON BONAPARTE
(1769–1821)
was born in Corsica. He became an
army officer in 1785, and after rapid
promotion, took command of the
army of the interior in 1795. After
a coup in 1799, Napoleon became
first consul, and in 1804 emperor.
Between 1804 and 1810 he consolidated his empire in Europe. In 1809
he nullified his 13-year marriage to
Josephine and married Marie Louise
of Austria, who bore him a son. In
1814, following defeat in Russia, he
abdicated and was banished to Elba.
In 1815 he reassumed power, but was
crushed at the Battle of Waterloo
and exiled to St. Helena, where he
died in 1821.

MARIE-JOSEPHE-ROSE (JOSEPHINE)
TASCHER DE LA PAGERIE
(1763–1814)
grew up on the island of Martinique.
In 1779 she married the wealthy
Vicomte de Beauharnais, and moved
to Paris. They had two children—
Hortense and Eugène—but the
couple separated. She met the young
Napoleon in 1795, and they married
the following year. She was crowned
empress in 1804, but Napoleon
nullified the marriage in 1809. She
retreated to Malmaison, where she
died in 1814.

Above *Josephine's bedroom at Malmaison, decorated in
sumptuous style during the height of Napoleon's influence in
France. This was where the empress felt most relaxed and at
home. The bed and most of the furniture bear her monogram.*

weeping when Napoleon was away leading military
campaigns. But Napoleon saw things very differently.
From his point of view,

> "the wife was made for the husband, the husband for
> his country, his family, and glory."

In March 1807 he wrote to her,

> "All my life long I have sacrificed everything to
> my destiny—peace of mind, personal advantage,
> happiness."

On December 15, 1809, Napoleon had his marriage
to Josephine annulled. She retired to Malmaison, her
private and best-loved residence. The letters that

Napoleon wrote to her there just after the annulment reveal tenderness and his sense of loss. He told
how he had visited one of their palaces, the Tuileries, scene of the street battle in October 1795 that
first brought them together:

> "That great palace seemed empty to me and I felt
> lost in it."

In April 1814 Napoleon was forced to abdicate
with his dreams of empire in ruins about him. The
following month Josephine died at age 51. Although
Josephine came to love her husband with a single-
minded devotion, the intense passion in this relationship was always Napoleon's. In his final exile on
St. Helena, Napoleon wrote:

> "Josephine is the only woman I have ever truly
> loved. She reigns in my heart and I mourn for her."

Ludwig van Beethoven to the "Immortal Beloved"

c. 1811–12
Good morning, on July 7th

Even when I am in bed my thoughts rush to you, my eternally beloved, now and then joyfully, then again sadly, waiting to know whether Fate will hear our prayer—To face life I must live altogether with you or never see you. Yes, I am resolved to be a wanderer abroad until I can fly to your arms and say that I have found my true home with you and enfolded in your arms can let my soul be wafted to the realm of blessed spirits—alas, unfortunately it must be so— You will become composed, the more so as you know that I am faithful to you; no other woman can ever possess my heart—never—never—Oh God, why must one be separated from her who is so dear. Yet my life in V[ienna] at present is a miserable life—Your love has made me both the happiest and the unhappiest of mortals— At my age I now need stability and regularity in my life—can this coexist with our relationship?— Angel, I have just heard that the post goes every day—and therefore I must close, so that you may receive the letter immediately—Be calm; for only by calmly considering our lives can we achieve our purpose to live together—Be calm—love me—Today—yesterday—what tearful longing for you—for you—you—my life—my all—all good wishes to you—Oh, do continue to love me—never misjudge your lover's most faithful heart.

> *ever yours*
>
> *ever mine*
>
> *ever ours.*

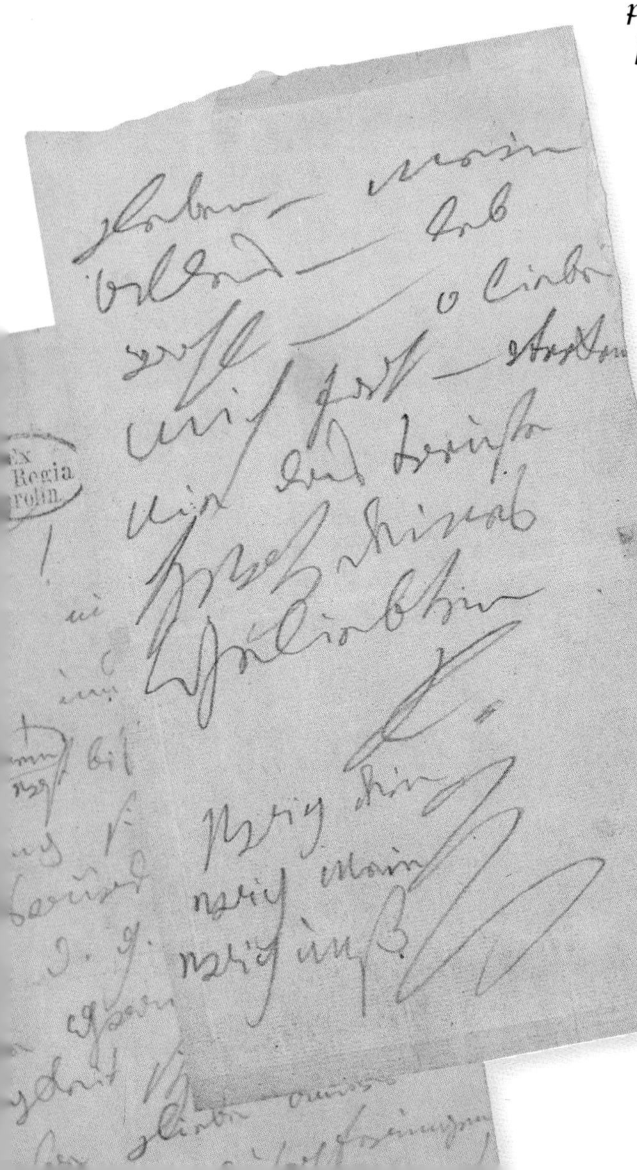

Ludwig van Beethoven never married. Any thoughts he had of marrying (and there were at least three women he is known to have felt strongly for) came to nothing. After his death in 1827, a letter, written in three sections, was found in a drawer. It was addressed to the "Immortal Beloved," but appears never to have been sent. The third part of the letter is printed opposite. It was dated July 7, but no year was given. Beethoven scholars generally think that it was probably written in either 1811 or 1812. No one knows who the "Immortal Beloved" was, but it seems fitting that a brooding musical genius should have left behind passionate words to a mysterious muse.

Beethoven was born in 1770 in Bonn, Germany, into a poor but musical family. By 1800, when he finished his *First Symphony,* he already had a considerable reputation as a concert pianist. But the onset of deafness in 1798 brought with it painful emotional isolation. In his *Heiligenstadt Testament,* written to his two brothers but never sent to them, he says:

"As the autumn leaves wither and fall, so has my own life become barren."

Forced by increasing deafness to turn away from the concert platform where he had excelled, Beethoven became increasingly absorbed in composing, and would walk for hours at a time in the countryside around Vienna slowly thinking through themes for new works. Although he had female friends, he seemed troubled by an indecisiveness about women, perhaps even by a fear of them. By aligning the descriptions of all those he seemed to be attracted to, the ideal he sought but shied away from can be reconstructed. Such a woman would have been beautiful, younger than he was, well placed in society, cultured, and musical. Inevitably, as a composer earning a living through teaching piano and musical composition to

Above *Ludwig van Beethoven, painted in oils by Joseph Willibrord Mähler in 1815.*

aristocratic patrons, he came into contact with many attractive and sometimes eligible women. But he is on record as saying that he,

> *"...knew of no marriage in which one or the other did not regret the step after a time,"*

and that he was pleased that none of the few women whom he really admired during his life ever became his wife. Nonetheless, a close friend remembered that he,

> *"...loved to see women, particularly pretty, youthful faces."*

It is a poignant reminder of the difficult balance between great artistic endeavor and everyday happiness that a man so full of passionate feeling should be so guarded where love was concerned.

There is no way of knowing from Beethoven's letter what the "Immortal Beloved" looked like, but clearly he was addressing a real person, not an idealized vision. In the first part of the letter, not printed here, Beethoven used her own pencil

Above *The first edition of Beethoven's* An die ferne Geliebte *(To my distant beloved) published in 1816. That same year, Beethoven spoke to a music tutor of a "hopeless love" five years earlier. The remark has caused some experts to link the song cycle to the "Immortal Beloved."*

to write to her, he gave details of his dreadful journey, discussed the times of the post and spoke about a probable meeting with her. There was, then, a woman to whom Beethoven wrote declaring an intense passion. But who was she? And did he send her a copy of the letter, or were his words read by no one but himself until after his death? The letter is both a powerful testimony of love and an unsolved puzzle. It has intrigued the admiring devotees of Beethoven ever since it was first discovered.

There have been many theories about the identity of the "Immortal Beloved." Some experts favor Countess Josephine Deym, whom Beethoven fell in love with after she was widowed in 1804 at the age of 25. Between 1804 and 1807 he wrote her numerous love letters, 14 of which have survived. However, some of the evidence in the three-part letter points away from Josephine. It was intended for a woman Beethoven knew well and loved after they had known each other for some time, rather than on impulse. He expressed a need for stability in his life, and though he clearly wanted to live with her, faced an obstacle. At this point all becomes speculative. It seems likely that the "Immortal Beloved" was married,

Below *Bad Teplitz, the spa town outside Vienna where Beethoven went for a cure in the summers of 1811 and 1812, and where he wrote two parts of the three-part letter to the "Immortal Beloved."*

Above *Antonie Brentano, the most likely of three women who may have been Beethoven's "Immortal Beloved." She was a married woman and a close friend.* **Below left** *Josephine Deym (née von Brunsvik) was a former love and a long-standing friend.* **Below right** *Dorothea Ertmann was a talented pianist, to whom Beethoven gave lessons.*

and that she lived in Vienna, as Beethoven did. She was visiting a town with the initial K, probably Karlsbad. The police register at Karlsbad records four women visitors in late June and early July 1812. The 55-year-old Elizabeth von der Recke came with her lover, Christopher Tiedge. Baroness Dorothea Ertmann arrived on June 25 to seek a cure, and she fits the description: charming, young, and a fine pianist. Beethoven began giving her lessons in 1803, and she became one of the greatest interpreters of his sonatas. She lived near him in Vienna until 1824. Princess Moritz Liechtenstein, reputed to be "Vienna's most beautiful woman," was at Karlsbad with her husband during this period, as was the most likely candidate, Antonie von Brentano.

Antonie Birkenstock was born in Vienna in 1780, and married Franz Brentano, a merchant from Frankfurt, in 1798. The couple lived in Vienna with their six children from 1809 to 1812, where they became close friends with Beethoven. The composer joined them on holiday in Karlsbad in 1812, and may have taken the opportunity to declare his love to Antonie in writing. Soon after their return to Vienna, the Brentanos moved back to Frankfurt, but they continued to correspond with Beethoven, and Franz lent him sums of money, without expecting a return. In 1823 Beethoven dedicated the *Diabelli Variations* to her. If she was his "Immortal Beloved," emotion expressed through music may have been his most eloquent declaration of passionate love.

The
❦ *L o v e r s* ❦

LUDWIG VAN BEETHOVEN
(1770–1827)
showed so much talent as a child musician that he turned professional at the age of 11. As a young man he was taught by Mozart and Haydn and his virtuoso performances on the piano attracted aristocratic patrons in Vienna, the musical center of Europe. Beethoven is reputed to be the first musician to make a living from private patronage, without subsidies from the church or court. His best-known works (the Symphonies numbers 2 through 8, the *Moonlight Sonata*, the *Battle Symphony*, and his only opera, *Fidelio*) were written in his thirties and forties, when he was already suffering from deafness. He told friends that his affliction hampered him least when he was playing and composing, and most when he was in company. By the time he was 50, his career was blighted by this handicap, but he went on composing despite the difficulties—the *Ninth Symphony* and several string quartets are from this period. When he died of dropsy at age 57, his last words were "Applause friends, the comedy is over."

THE "IMMORTAL BELOVED"
No one has ever identified her—she remains a romantic enigma.

Lord Byron to Teresa Guiccioli

Bologna, 25 August, 1819

My dearest Teresa,
I have read this book in your garden;— my love, you were absent, or else I could not have read it. It is a favourite book of yours, and the writer was a friend of mine. You will not understand these English words, and others will not understand them,—which is the reason I have not scrawled them in Italian. But you will recognize the handwriting of him who passionately loved you, and you will divine that, over a book which was yours, he could only think of love.

Above *Teresa Guiccioli—the last great love of Byron's life—at age 21, painted by William Edward West in 1822.*

In that word, beautiful in all languages, but most so in yours—Amor mio—is comprised my existence here and hereafter. I feel I exist here, and I feel I shall exist hereafter,—to what purpose you will decide; my destiny rests with you, and you are a woman, eighteen years of age, and two out of a convent. I wish that you had staid there, with all my heart,—or, at least, that I had never met you in your married state.

But all this is too late. I love you, and you love me,— at least, you say so, and act as if you did so, which last is a great consolation in all events. But I more than love you, and cannot cease to love you.

Think of me, sometimes, when the Alps and ocean divide us,—but they never will, unless you wish it.

Lord Byron.

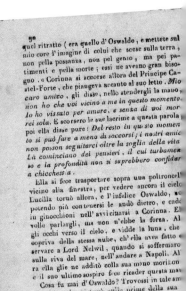

Right *Byron's love letter, written at the back of Teresa's copy of the novel, Corinne, by Mme. de Staël.*

Romantic novelists have long portrayed the dissipated aristocrat whose heart is awakened to true love by an innocent girl. It was played out in real life, at a deeper and more touching level than in fiction, by Lord Byron and the 18-year-old Teresa, Countess Guiccioli. The letter printed here was written a few months after their meeting and reflects his emotional state: perplexed, but touched by the hope of a new beginning.

When Byron met Teresa in Venice early in April 1819, he was one of the most famous men in Europe: the admired author of fine lyric poems and blistering satires, a notorious lover, and a liberal political sympathizer. He separated from his first wife, Annabella Milbanke—whom he married on January 2, 1815—after less than a year. Some claimed she walked out on him because he had an affair with his half-sister, Augusta Leigh. This, coupled with gossip about his many affairs, and his savage attacks on the British government, drove him from England in 1816, no longer welcomed among the English aristocracy.

He went first to Switzerland, spending much time with the poet Percy Bysshe Shelley and his admirers. After Switzerland he spent two years of restless promiscuity in Venice, and by the age of 31 was gaining weight and losing his dark good looks.

A chance meeting with Teresa changed the course of his life. Last of his many loves, he behaved as if she were the first. The evening they met they talked excitedly of poetry, particularly that of Dante and Petrarch. The year before, Teresa, fresh out of convent school, had become the third wife of the rich and eccentric 60-year-old Count Guiccioli in a marriage of convenience. Not surprisingly, Byron disliked the count; but he warmed to Teresa's father, Count Gamba, and his son Pietro. Like Byron, they held strong political principles; they were deeply involved in the struggle to free northern Italy from Austrian oppression imposed by the treaty following Napoleon's recent defeat.

In Italian custom there was a place for a discreet attendant, a "gentleman servant," in a marriage of convenience such as Teresa's. But although he could pay court to her, the role excluded public recognition of them as a couple. This was not enough for Byron. He wanted a relationship that was lasting. As Teresa put it, he was:

> "…not a man to confine himself to sentiment. And the first step taken, there was no further obstacle in the following days."

Breaking all the rules established by aristocratic Italian society, the couple spent 10 days together, openly, in Venice. This was no casual liaison for Byron. As he wrote to a friend,

> "What shall I do? I am in love, and tired of promiscuous concubinage, and have now an opportunity of settling for life."

Invited to visit Ravenna by Count Alessandro Guiccioli, Byron took up lodgings near Teresa's home and became a part of the household, riding with her every day under the pines, and writing some of the best poetry of his life in his epic, *Don Juan*. He wrote the letter printed here in English, a language he knew Teresa did

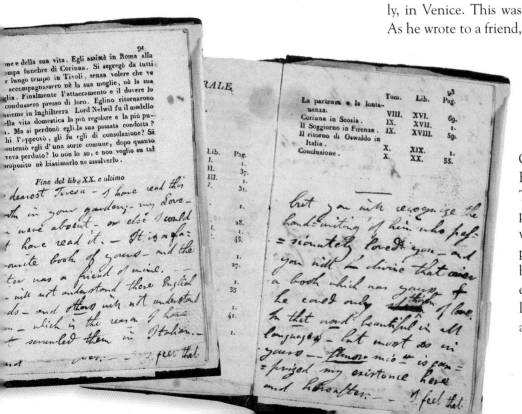

not understand, in her copy of their friend Madame de Staël's sentimental novel *Corinne*. He would not translate his words for her, writing almost as though to himself. She could only have understood the two words "*Amor mio*"—"my love."

As the love between Byron and Teresa deepened, so his friendship with her father and brother grew. They initiated him into the secret revolutionary society, the Carbonari, to which he gave money for arms. This activity was closely monitored by the Austrian police, and in 1821 the Gambas were exiled from Ravenna. Teresa was by now seeking a separation from her husband, and she and Byron accompanied them.

The following year, in Genoa, an unfriendly spy spread an unkind rumor:

> "*It is said that he is already sated or tired of Favorite, the Guiccioli. He has…expressed his intention of going to Athens in order to make himself adored by the Greeks.*"

In fact, Byron's energies, reinvigorated by his love for Teresa, now turned from the cause of Italy—where police scrutiny rendered him powerless—to that of Greece. As a young man he had wept to see the state of the country under its Turkish masters; now, after

400 years of enslavement, the Greeks were up in arms and he longed to help. In December 1823 he arrived at Missolonghi in western Greece, with plans to capture a fortress held by the Turks. Instead fever struck him down, and on April 19, 1824, he died, murmuring in delirium that there were,

> "*…things which make the world dear to me.*"

Was the image of Teresa in his mind? She believed so. All her life she defended his memory, and on her own deathbed she wrote,

> "*The more Byron is known, the better he will be loved.*"

In her copy of *Corinne* she had underlined the words of his letter and written simply,

> "*God bless him.*"

Right George Gordon, sixth Lord Byron—a Romantic libertarian all his life—in Albanian costume as Childe Harold, the hero of his epic poem Childe Harold's Pilgrimage.

❧ *T h e   L o v e r s* ❧

GEORGE GORDON, LORD BYRON (1788–1824), English Romantic poet and satirist, was brought up in poverty in Scotland. At the age of 10 he inherited his great-uncle's title and property, and moved to Newstead Abbey, England. Byron was educated at Harrow and later Cambridge. Travels in Greece resulted in the sardonic poem *Childe Harold's Pilgrimage*. In January 1815 he married Annabella Milbanke, who bore him a daughter, Augusta, and then left him. Rumor named his relationship with his half-sister, Augusta Leigh, as the cause, and Byron was ostracized. He sold Newstead and began a debauched life in Italy, often in the company of the poet Shelley and his friends. One of these was Claire Clairmont, the mother of Byron's daughter Allegra. During 1818–23, years spent with Teresa Guiccioli, he wrote three cantos of *Don Juan*, a satirical romance, *The Prophecy of Dante*, and four poetic

dramas. Longing to help Greece obtain independence from Turkey, he joined their fight in December 1823, but died of fever on April 19, 1824. Refused burial in Westminster Abbey, he is buried with his ancestors near Newstead Abbey.

TERESA GUICCIOLI (1801–73), born Teresa Gamba Ghiselli, was the daughter of Count Gamba, a nobleman from Ravenna in Italy. Teresa had a good convent-school education, and at 17 was married—in a marriage of convenience—to 60-year-old Count Alessandro Guiccioli as his third wife. She separated from him at the height of her passionate affair with Byron, and went to live with her father and brother, whose political views had earned them exile in Pisa. In 1851, 27 years after Byron's death, Teresa married the French Marquis de Boissy and in 1868 wrote (in French) her recollections: *Lord Byron Judged by the Witnesses of his Life*.

Above Teresa and Count Alessandro Guiccioli's palazzo in Ravenna. It was here, from 1819 to 1821, that Byron courted Teresa, under her husband's ambivalent but watchful eye.

Franz Liszt *to* Marie d'Agoult

December 1834

Marie! Marie!

Oh let me repeat that name a hundred times,
*   a thousand times over;*
for three days now it has lived within me, oppressed me,
*   set me afire.*
I am not writing to you, no, I am close beside you. I see you,
*   I hear you…*
Eternity in your arms…Heaven, hell,
*   all is within you and even more than all…*
Oh! Leave me free to rave in my delirium.
Mean, cautious, narrow reality is no longer
enough for me.
We must live our lives to the full,
*   our loves, our sorrows…!*
Oh! you believe me capable of
*   self-sacrifice, chastity, temperance*
*   and piety, do you not?*
But let no more be said of this…
*   it is for you to question, to draw*
*   conclusions,*
*   to save me as you see fit.*
Let me be mad, senseless
*   since you can do nothing, nothing*
*   at all for me.*
It is good for me to speak to you now.
This is to be! To be!!!

Right *Franz Liszt by*
Henri Lehmann, 1839.

One evening in late 1832, or early the next year, the young Hungarian pianist Franz Liszt arrived at the home of a fashionable aristocrat, the Marquise La Vayer. There he met Marie d'Agoult, a 27-year-old countess, icily beautiful, but unhappily married and the mother of two young daughters. In her Memoirs, Marie described the man she saw,

> " …a tall figure, excessively thin, a pale face with great sea-green eyes in which glistened swift flashes of light like waves catching the sunlight…features at once suffering and powerful."

Their meeting began 10 years of passion, joy, and bitterness for them both. Liszt's letter, written sometime in 1834 and reproduced here, captures the conflicting emotions that later consumed them.

Above *Marie d'Agoult in 1843, by Henri Lehmann, one of the leading portrait painters of the time and a close friend of Liszt and Marie. Beside it (right) is the passionate letter Liszt wrote her, printed opposite.*

Marie, intelligent and sophisticated, was

> "six inches of snow covering twenty feet of lava,"

as a contemporary put it. She came from a family of wealthy bankers with a history of wild liaisons and mental instability. Despairing of finding a husband she liked among those her family thought acceptable, she simply decided to take the next one they offered. The comte Charles d'Agoult (1790–1875), a war-wounded army officer, was 15 years her senior, kind, and self-effacing to the point of invisibility. Realizing how different Marie was from him, he offered her freedom from the marriage, should she ever want it. The 21-year-old Liszt seemed to offer her a reason for accepting the generous offer.

Soon Marie and Liszt were meeting regularly. As lovers they had much to offer each other: for Liszt, the security of Marie's wealth, the glitter of her connections, and the intimate and loving audience an artist craves; and for Marie, possession of a man who captivated everybody, a genius for her to inspire. In Europe, rich wives often took lovers. That her lover was a musician, a paid servant of the salons from some obscure village in Hungary, added drama to scandal. It broke not only the bonds of marriage but the boundaries of class as well.

However, there were misgivings. In September 1834, Liszt went to Brittany to stay with a friend, a priest named the Abbé Lamennais. In this quiet retreat, Liszt confronted the conflict within him, his private, meditative side against the public, passionate pianist. Then in October, Marie's elder daughter, six-year-old Louise, took ill and died after two fevered months. Marie was so overwrought that when her other small daughter Claire tried to console her, she abruptly sent her off to a convent to be cared for by others. Liszt wrote anxious letters. Marie did not reply. But when they met again early in 1835, they put aside their hesitations; when Marie found she was pregnant, they decided to elope. To avoid the worst effects of scandal and to find creative solitude, they moved to Switzerland. Parisians joked that Liszt carried her off in a piano.

On May 26, Marie wrote to her husband from Switzerland:

> "*I have no wrongs to reproach you with, you have always been full of affection and devotion for me; you have always thought of me, never of yourself, and yet I have been truly unhappy.*"

This was her only apology. She was leaving him. He stayed at home and raised their daughter Claire, until she, in turn, married and claimed the family home. Charles d'Agoult lived out his last years in lodgings in Paris.

Marie and Liszt, still not married, began a life of many addresses, in Switzerland, Italy, France, and Germany. But they were most happy early in their relationship in Italy, where two of their three children were born. In September 1837, Liszt advised the young poet, Louis de Ronchaud,

> "*When you write the story of two happy lovers, place them on the shores of Lake Como.*"

But it was there at Bellagio that Marie also began to suffer nervous fears, remorse, and self-doubt. Could she sustain the role she had taken on, to shelter Liszt

Above *The gardens of the Villa Melzi, Bellagio, on the shores of Lake Como, where Liszt and Marie spent many happy days from September to November, 1837. Liszt was working on his* Grandes Etudes *at the time.*

so that he could write his music? Entries in her diary express these anxieties with remarkable frankness.

> "*I feel myself an obstacle to his life; I'm no good to him. I cast sadness and discouragement over his days.*"

She had underestimated his need to exhaust himself at the piano, to court and overwhelm an audience. In response to the public's urgings, his career as the greatest virtuoso pianist the world had ever seen gathered pace, concert after concert, town after town, from Lisbon to Moscow, from Cork to Constantinople. A frenzy of performances separated him from Marie for months on end, and rumors linked him with other women. Behind each triumph Marie sensed, sometimes correctly, an infidelity. Her bitterness engulfed them both. In 1839, after relations between them had broken down, Marie returned to Paris. Liszt wrote from Utrecht in December 1842:

"The day is cold and dark. The only ray that comes to me, the sole source of light and warmth, is my memory of you, dear Marie. I think back to our awakenings in Como and Florence…I feel I have forgotten how to live."

The final break came in 1844, when rumors linked Liszt with the dancer Lola Montez. The affair almost certainly never happened, but the damage was nonetheless done. Marie wrote,

"I am willing to be your mistress, but not one of your mistresses,"

and communication between them broke down.

Seventeen years later, they met again in Paris. Marie, who had written a novel based on her life with Liszt, was a figure in Parisian society. Liszt was living with Princess Carolyne Sayn-Wittgenstein. He still triumphed in Europe, celebrated as a composer as well as a performer. Liszt kissed his former lover and, referring to spiritual roots that Marie had never begun to understand, said:

"Marie, let me use the language of a simple country-man. God bless you. Wish me no evil."

It was their last meeting. She told a friend,

"It is still he, and he alone, who makes me feel the divine mystery of life. With his departure I feel the emptiness around me and I shed tears."

❧ The Lovers ❧

FRANZ LISZT
(1811–86)
was a Hungarian-born child prodigy who grew up to become one of the most influential composers of the 19th century. By the age of six he was displaying exceptional musical ability. He gave his first concert at the age of 9, and by 11 had published his first piano piece and performed in Vienna before some of Europe's most eminent musicians. As a teenager he took Paris society by storm with his virtuosity and remarkable skill in sight-reading and improvisation. Of his 700 and more compositions, perhaps his most important works are the *Piano Sonata in B Minor*, the *Dante Symphony*, and the *Faust Symphony*. He had two great loves in his life, Comtesse Marie d'Agoult, and later Princess Carolyne Sayn-Wittgenstein. A man of strong religious feeling, passion, and intelligence he ended his life as a cleric in minor orders, dying at 74 at Bayreuth in Bavaria.

MARIE DE FLAVIGNY,
COMTESSE D'AGOULT
(1805–76)
was descended from German bankers and minor French aristocrats. She was Liszt's mistress for 10 years. A competent writer, she is best known for her novel *Nélida*—a thinly disguised account of her relationship with Liszt—which she wrote using the pen name Daniel Stern. The hero of the book fails to fulfill himself as an artist after the end of a long affair, but is reunited with his lover on his deathbed and dies in her arms. Cosima, the second of Marie's three children by Liszt and the only one to survive to old age, married the composer Richard Wagner.

Above *In 1842, when Liszt visited Berlin, "Lisztomania" swept the city. The hero-worship of his fans bordered on hysteria, as this contemporary caricature shows.*

Right *The opening bars of Liszt's* Huguenots Fantasia, *the only work that he dedicated to Marie d'Agoult.*

Victor Hugo to Juliette Drouet

December 31st, 1851

You have been wonderful, my Juliette, all through these dark and violent days. If I needed love, you brought it to me, bless you! When, in my hiding-places, always dangerous, after a night of waiting, I heard the key of my door trembling in your fingers, peril and darkness were no longer round me—what entered then was light! We must never forget those terrible, but so sweet, hours when you were close to me in the intervals of fighting. Let us remember all our lives that dark little room, the ancient hangings, the two armchairs, side by side, the meal we ate off the corner of the table, the cold chicken you had brought; our sweet converse, your caresses, your anxieties, your devotion. You were surprised to find me calm and serene. Do you know whence came both calmness and serenity? From you....

Above *Juliette Drouet, age 26, from a lithograph by Léon Noël made in 1832, a year before she met Hugo. Nineteen years later he wrote her this letter (**right**).*

Victor Hugo, the 19th-century French writer, wrote the letter extracted here soon after his mistress, Juliette Drouet, had risked her life to save his. He possessed an apparently boundless energy for writing, politics, good food, and beautiful women. And he indulged all of his enthusiasms. During his lifetime he won public adulation for his novels and poetry, as well as for his revolutionary thinking about freedom. His reputation reached such a height that, when he died in Paris, some two million people followed his coffin, and a day of national mourning was declared. This extraordinary man shared this colorful life with his wife, Adèle Foucher, and a long succession of mistresses, the most important of whom was the renowned beauty, Juliette Drouet.

Above *Victor Hugo, photographed by his son Charles in Jersey (one of the Channel Islands) during the period 1853-55. In exile from the French mainland, Hugo spent much of his time on the British-owned but French-speaking islands.*

Victor met Juliette in 1833, the year he married Adèle. Both women stayed with him for the rest of their lives, Adèle as wife, Juliette as mistress, secretary, and nurse. She was 26 when they met—Hugo was 30—an aspiring actress with a string of wealthy lovers, rehearsing as Princess Negroni, a minor part in one of Hugo's plays, *Lucrèce Borgia*. The role offered her few lines, but Juliette gave it beauty, wit, elegance, and a striking stage presence. From the first she fed Hugo's vanity, announcing:

"There is no such thing as a minor role in a play by Monsieur Victor Hugo."

They began a passionate affair, revolving around her complete devotion to him. Juliette gave up her glittering social life and rich lovers, the stage and friends, and lived on an allowance provided by Hugo. She seldom went out, and accounted to Hugo for everything she spent. She passed her days copying his writings, and reading his poems. They took holidays together in France, Belgium, Holland, Germany, and the Swiss Alps. Adèle, whose tears and protests

were ignored by Victor, continued to make public appearances as his wife. In truth, though, she had taken a lover herself. A year later, Hugo and Juliette were together in Juliette's native Brittany when Adèle wrote:

"I do believe that in spite of everything, you love me, and that you are enjoying yourself, since you are in no hurry to return. Truth to tell, these two certainties make me happy...."

As time passed both Victor's writing and his career prospered. In 1841 he was elected to the French Academy. He became a deputy for Paris, first in the Constituent Assembly and then in the Legislative Assembly. Throughout this period his affairs with other women were plentiful and, unknown to Juliette, in 1844 he took another important mistress, Léonie D'Aunet. Adèle became friendly with Léonie, seeing her as a potential ally against Juliette. Seven years later, however, Victor began to find Léonie an embarrassment and the relationship waned. In retaliation for his coolness, in June 1851 Léonie sent all the letters Victor had written her to Juliette. Not only were they similar to letters Juliette herself had received over the previous 18 years, but also their receipt marked Juliette's first knowledge of her rival.

When Juliette confronted Victor, he admitted everything and offered a

Right Léonie D'Aunet, another of Victor's many mistresses, and Juliette's main rival for his affections. Léonie and Hugo caused a scandal in 1845, the year after they met, but Juliette, who led a reclusive life, was unaware of the affair until 1851.

solution that matched his vanity. He proposed a contest. Both women would continue as his mistress, and the one who showed him the most love would win his favors. The challenge was accepted. In her letter of June 28, 1851, Juliette wrote:

> *"In the name of all that you hold sacred, in the name of my great grief, beloved, do not show any false generosity to me; do not tear your heart in pieces merely to spare mine….Have pity upon me, dear God, spare me this last drop of bitterness which I must drink in seeing suffer through my fault the man whom I love better than life, better than happiness….O God! let him be happy with another rather than unhappy with me…."*

Léonie, in contrast, resented the terms of the contest from the beginning and objected to the sacrifices demanded by Victor. Youth and beauty were on Léonie's side, but Juliette, happy to bear any humiliation for Victor's sake, won the advantage.

In the wider world of politics Louis-Napoléon (president of the Second Republic from 1850–52, and then emperor of the French, as Napoleon III, 1852–71) was bidding to assume absolute power. Victor vigorously opposed him. In December 1851, Louis-Napoléon launched his coup d'état and Victor Hugo became a wanted man, in hiding, his life in danger. Amid the slaughter on the streets, while Adèle was sick and could do little to help, Juliette found safe houses for him, arranged false papers to

Below Rioting on the streets of Paris in 1848, and the burning of the Chateau d'Eau by the mob, from a painting by Hagnauer. It was scenes such as this that prompted Juliette to arrange Hugo's escape from the capital.

The Lovers

VICTOR-MARIE HUGO (1802–85) was born in Besançon, France, the third son of an army general. He was a sickly infant and was not expected to live, but grew more robust from the age of two when he went to live with his mother in Paris—"the birthplace of my soul." As a teenager he began to fill notebooks with poetry. In maturity he was a prolific and very successful poet, dramatist, and novelist, and the most celebrated author of his generation. His most famous works include *The Hunchback of Notre Dame* (1831), *Les Chants du Crepuscule* (1835) and *Les Misérables* (1862). Victor Hugo had an enormous appetite for women, work, food, and wine. He was also passionately interested in politics, an anti-Bonapartist, and an international spokesman for liberty in 19th-century Europe. He is buried beside Voltaire and Rousseau in the Panthéon in Paris.

JULIETTE DROUET (1806–83) was born Julienne Josephine Gauvain in Brest, France, and took her uncle's name Drouet as a child when he adopted her after her parents died. Though literacy among women was rare in her day, she could read and write at the age of 5, and by the age of 10 she showed a great aptitude for literature and poetry. At 16 she became a painter's model and an aspiring actress, taking the stage name Juliette. For a while she was supported by a succession of rich and talented lovers. At 19 she had a daughter by the distinguished sculptor James Pradier. Meeting Victor Hugo transformed her life. She devoted herself to him for 50 years, without the security of being married to him. During the last six weeks of her life, when she was dying from cancer, Hugo never left her side. She died in his arms at the age of 77, while he was kissing her.

get him out of the country and then, discreetly, followed him into exile, first to Belgium, then to the Channel Islands. Léonie was forgotten in the confusion. On December 31, 1851, Hugo wrote the letter extracted here to the woman who had saved his life.

In exile for 20 years until Napoleon III fell from power, Victor Hugo became a symbol of intellectual resistance to tyranny. In his heroic old age Juliette acted as a secretary-companion and worshiper, living near, but apart from, the Hugo family. Not until 1867 did Adèle, realizing that she was dying, make peace with the woman who had shared her husband for so many years. In the final months of her life, Adèle admitted Juliette into the Hugo family circle. Juliette wrote that she was:

> *"overjoyed, moved, dazzled, and happier than a poor old woman has any right to be."*

Adèle died in 1868 and Juliette became Victor's publicly acknowledged partner, a wife in all but name.

Following the proclamation of the Third Republic in 1871 Hugo and Juliette returned to Paris where

Hugo was regarded as a public hero and guardian of liberty. For a short time he agreed to play a part in public affairs by serving as a deputy in the National Assembly, but he found the work too arduous and resigned after the first month in order to live a quiet life with Juliette. He was subsequently elected a senator by the people of Paris, and on his 80th birthday the street where he lived, Avenue d'Eylau, was renamed Avenue Victor Hugo in his honor.

When Juliette died in 1883 Victor never fully recovered from the loss. He outlived her by two years, but he never wrote again, an indication of just how much Juliette's quiet devotion over the years had meant to him.

Above *A detail of the decoration originally done for the Chinese drawing room of Juliette's home on Guernsey in the Channel Islands. The room was designed by Victor for Juliette, and the motifs on the walls incorporate her initials.*

Left *Victor's pen, sepia-wash and charcoal picture, dominated by the couple's intertwined initials (V. H. and J. D.). Beneath them is a sketch of the Hugo family home at Marine Terrace, Jersey.*

Below *An original illustration of the character Cossette from Hugo's most famous novel* Les Misérables. *It was written in exile during the regime of Napoleon III and published in 1862. The novel makes heroes of the antigovernment forces.*

Lord Randolph Churchill to Jennie Jerome

August 1873

I cannot keep myself from writing any longer to you dearest, although I have not had any answer to either of my two letters. I suppose your mother does not allow you to write to me. Perhaps you have not got either of my letters...I am so dreadfully afraid that perhaps you may think I am forgetting you. I can assure you dearest Jeannette you have not been out of my thoughts hardly for one minute since I left you Monday. I have written to my father everything, how much I love you how much I long & pray & how much I wld sacrifice if it were necessary to be married to you and to live ever after with you...I shall [not] get an answer till Monday & whichever way it lies I shall go to Cowes soon after & tell your mother everything. I am afraid she does not like me vy much from what I have heard...I wld do anything she wished if she only wld not oppose us. Dearest if you are as fond of me as I am of you...nothing human cld keep us long apart. This last week has seemed an eternity to me; Oh, I wld give my soul for another of those days we had together not long ago...Oh if I cld only get one line from you to reassure me, but I dare not ask you to do anything that your mother wld disapprove of or has perhaps forbidden you to do...Sometimes I doubt so I cannot help it whether you really like me as you said at Cowes you did. If you do I cannot fear for the future tho' difficulties may lie in our way only to be surmounted by patience.

Goodbye dearest Jeannette. My first and only love...Believe me ever to be

Yrs devotedly and lovingly,
Randolf S. Churchill

Above *Lady Randolph Churchill, in a sketch by John Sargent, who captured the glamour of Victorian society.*

On August 12, 1873, 24-year-old Lord Randolph Churchill, youngest son of the duke of Marlborough, attended a ball given for the future tsar of Russia aboard H.M.S. *Ariadne*. The ship was moored off the fashionable English yachting resort of Cowes on the Isle of Wight, just off the south coast of England, and there Randolph met 19-year-old Jennie Jerome, a dark-haired, dark-eyed, and beautiful American.

The spirited and accomplished Jennie had been brought up in Paris by her mother, Clara, who was entranced by the social life of the French capital. But in 1870 the Franco-Prussian war broke out; Paris sank into gloom and the Jeromes left France for London to enjoy the social events of the summer. There, Jennie was presented to the prince and princess of Wales. The Jeromes then moved on to Cowes.

Lord Randolph was no dancer; after the first quadrille, he and Jennie sat and talked for the rest of the ball. It was a rare, mutual, and apparently genuine occurrence of love at first sight. The ball ended in the early evening, and Jennie persuaded her mother to ask Randolph back to dinner. Before the night was over he told a friend that he meant to marry "the dark one." Jennie, too, told her sister that she had a presentiment she would marry Randolph. Her sister laughed, but when Randolph proposed as they took a garden stroll the following evening, Jennie accepted him without hesitation.

Their parents were not pleased. Mrs. Jerome would not hear of so sudden an engagement; the duke of Marlborough thought Jennie's father, Leonard—a New York stockbroker—sounded like:

"a sporting, and I should think vulgar kind of man."
A week after the ball, Mrs. Jerome and Jennie returned to Paris as planned. Randolph bombarded his love with adoring letters such as the one extracted here. At first she was forbidden to reply. But by winter and throughout the following spring, letters flew between England and Paris, where Jennie was trying to pacify her mother while assuring Randolph,

"I could leave Father, Mother and the whole world for you if it were necessary."
From New York, Mr. Jerome wrote to his daughter,

"I always thought if you ever did fall in love it would be a dangerous affair. You were never born to love lightly."
Randolph finally put sufficient pressure on his parents, hinting that he would not be a candidate for the local parliamentary constituency of Woodstock unless they allowed him to marry Jennie. His gamble paid off. In the General Election of February 1874, Randolph won Woodstock by 65 votes, and on April 15 he married Jennie in the chapel of the British Embassy in Paris.

Once married, and immediately pregnant, Jennie discovered that the family tensions within Blenheim Palace—the Marlborough's vast and drafty dwelling place near Oxford—needed careful handling. She provided a much-needed calming influence on Randolph's hair-trigger temper. After the premature birth of her son Winston on November 30, 1874 (neither cradle nor baby clothes were ready), life became

Above *Jennie and Randolph photographed together in 1874, the year of their marriage.*

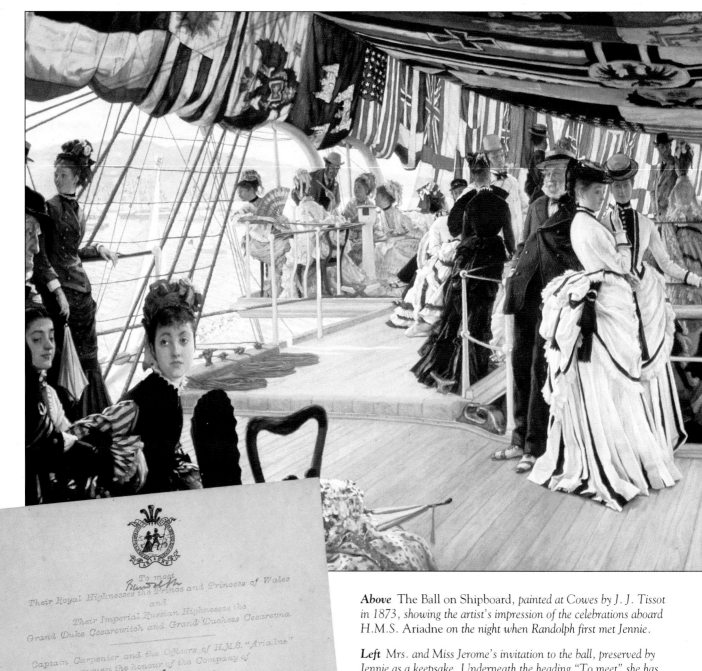

Above The Ball on Shipboard, *painted at Cowes by J. J. Tissot in 1873, showing the artist's impression of the celebrations aboard* H.M.S. Ariadne *on the night when Randolph first met Jennie.*

Left *Mrs. and Miss Jerome's invitation to the ball, preserved by Jennie as a keepsake. Underneath the heading "To meet" she has written in the word "Randolph."*

more exciting. The couple were welcomed into the brilliant social scene that centered on Queen Victoria's son, Edward, prince of Wales. Then Randolph upset everything.

To prevent his even more reckless brother, Blandford, from being cited in a divorce case, Randolph virtually blackmailed the prince, threatening to reveal compromising letters written by the prince to Lady Aylesford, the woman with whom Blandford was involved. The Aylesford Affair brought Lord Randolph close to fighting a duel with the prince, upset Queen Victoria, and split English high society. Jennie supported Randolph, and for his sake gave up much of the glittering life she loved.

The Churchills shifted their formidable energies into politics. Jennie campaigned for Randolph in elections; a contemporary song celebrated her canvassing, wearing a bonnet with pink roses:

*"And a smile that twinkled over
And that made a man most love her
Took the hearts and votes
of all Liberals in the town."*

Randolph's rise was so rapid, his oratory so sparkling and unpredictable, that everything seemed possible for them. In July 1886 "Randy," age 37, became simultaneously chancellor of the exchequer and leader of the House of Commons. He was widely discussed as the next Conservative prime minister.

Then, for the first time, Randolph's devotion to Jennie seemed to cool. She suspected an affair, but could not prove it. She herself was unswervingly faithful; her devoted admirer, Count Charles Kinsky, remained only a consoling friend as Randolph blighted his own career with another reckless move. Anxious to force through his financial policies, he offered his resignation. It was intended as a threat, like the one that had won him Jennie. Unexpectedly, the prime minister, Lord Salisbury, called his bluff and accepted his resignation.

Randolph never held high office again. Always an extravagant couple, they ran up debts as soon as his high income dwindled, and Randolph's behavior became ever more erratic. He suffered from a rare form of tumor on the brain, which medical science was unable to diagnose at the time. Modern medical techniques have recognized the malady, and also the serious affects of the drugs that he had been given over a long period. During his last years, the pain he suffered was agonizing. In her despair, Jennie finally turned to Count Kinsky. But Kinsky was the heir to a considerable estate, and his father had threatened to disinherit him if he did not marry the wife already chosen for him. On January 9, 1895, Kinsky married someone else. And on January 24 Randolph died, at

Right *"The finest view in England," Jennie wrote, on seeing Blenheim for the first time, "looking at the lake…and stately palace, I confess I felt awed. But my American pride forbade the admission."*

❦ *The Lovers* ❦

LORD RANDOLPH (HENRY SPENCER) CHURCHILL (1849–95), third son of the seventh duke of Marlborough, first entered the House of Commons in 1874—the same year he married Jennie—when he was just 25 years old. From 1876 to 1880 he was unofficial private secretary to his father, lord lieutenant (viceroy) of Ireland, actively supporting local self-government (but not Home Rule) for Ireland. In 1885 he was appointed secretary of state for India, and in 1886 chancellor of the exchequer and leader of the House of Commons. In December of that year, his resignation (a political ploy to push through his budget) was unexpectedly accepted. Illness in his last years resulted in a painful death at age 45.

JEANETTE (JENNIE) JEROME (1854–1921) was born in New York, one of three daughters to Leonard W. Jerome—a wealthy stockbroker—and Clara, an heiress. From 1868 Jennie lived in Paris, and in 1873, on a visit to England, was presented to the prince and princess of Wales. She married Lord Randolph in 1874, and bore him two sons, Winston—a future prime minister—and John. Five years after Randolph's death she married George Cornwallis-West, a 26-year-old officer in the Scots Guards. In 1912 they divorced; George married the actress Mrs. Patrick Campbell two years later. In 1918 Jennie married for a third time. She died in June 1921, and was buried beside Lord Randolph at Bladon, near Blenheim Palace.

age 45. In one month Jennie lost both a faithful friend and the only man to whom she had given her heart.

Sometimes a great love expresses itself best in its children. The brilliant English politician and his dazzling, generous-hearted American wife left a unique legacy: their son, Winston Churchill.

Henri Gaudier to Sophie Brzeska

November 16, 1912

Dearest and Best,
I went to the Zoo. The beasts had a curious effect on me, which I haven't hitherto experienced; I have always admired them, but now I hate them—the dreadful savagery of these wild animals who hurl themselves on their food is too horribly like the ways of humans. What moved me most was a group of four chimpanzees. They were like primitive men … It's most depressing thus to see our own origin—depressing, not because we sprang from this, but that we may so easily slip back to it. Our knowledge is great, but how empty!…[It] allows us to make use of all the forces already in existence—our art to interpret emotions already felt; a big war, an epidemic and we collapse into ignorance and darkness, fit sons of chimpanzees. Our one consolation is Love, confidence, the embracing of spirit and of body. When we are united we think neither of outer darkness nor of animal brutality. Our human superiority vibrates through our passions, and we love the world—but how insignificant we really are, and how subject to universal law!

Above *Sophie Brzeska. When Gaudier first met her he wrote "she has beauty à la Baudelaire" and an "enigmatic face."*

Sweet dear, I am so blessed in being able to love you, and blessed be the day when the great sun guided me to you; without your love I should have been flung into an outer darkness, where bones rot, and where man is subject to the same law as beasts … Dear, dear love, I press you to me with all my force, and only your help enables me to work. I thank you, dear Sun, lovely Star, for having created women and men that we may be united, mingle our personalities, melt together our hearts and, by the union of our passionate bodies, better liberate our souls, making of us a single creature—the absolute human which you have endowed with so many gifts.

Goodnight, dear heart, sweet Sister, Mother. Think that we are together in the same bed, and by our perfect union, making prayer to God.

Early in 1910 Sophie Brzeska, a highly strung and eccentric 38-year-old Polish woman, was sitting in the St. Geneviève Library in Paris, inventing imaginary lives for the people around her. By chance, a young aspiring artist, Henri Gaudier—only 18 years old—sat opposite her. Like Sophie, he had been in Paris just a few months and was lonely. But the unlikely couple were destined to share more, as the letter extracted here—written two years later in London—reveals. The curious relationship that developed was fueled by deep passion.

From childhood to the moment Henri met her, Sophie was a victim. To her weary mother, her womanizing father, and her eight brothers, she was a burden needing to be married off. She resisted, trying to stay focused on her own dream of writing. She fled Poland for Paris, where she accepted a succession of jobs as governess, one of which involved her living in the United States for several years. These ventures with other people's families left her contemplating suicide. Yet in June 1910 Henri saw her in a fresh light, describing her in a letter to a friend as,

> "...lithe and simple with a feline carriage and enigmatic face."

Henri saw Sophie through an artist's eyes. He delighted in her tempestuous voice, changing moods, and flashing eyes, at one moment tragic, the next lit with joy. From the age of six Henri had been interested in drawing, and encouraged by his carpenter father, had left his village to study art. In Paris he worked in a bookshop during the day and spent long evenings studying in the city's many libraries and museums. Sophie, acutely aware of his close proximity and famished for love, felt confused maternal longings for someone she could protect.

One night, as Henri walked Sophie home, he told her how he longed for someone who would understand him and encourage his ambitions. Sophie spontaneously replied,

> "I am too old for you really, but I will be a mother to you, if you agree."

Henri was charmed by the idea. They resolved to go together the next day to visit the Louvre. Nobody had ever listened to Henri as Sophie did in the galleries. They were extravagantly happy.

Severe poverty, however, made life in Paris difficult, and at the end of 1910—with Henri wanting to avoid military service—they moved to London. They decided to pass as brother and sister, changing their surnames to Gaudier-Brzeska. Still desperately poor, Sophie went so far as to beg for food in the street, cradling a doll wrapped up to look like a baby. Henri was outraged. When her meager savings ran

Right *The first page of Henri Gaudier's long letter to Sophie extracted opposite and (**far right**) Henri in his early 20's. Hunger and constant ill-health gave him a gaunt and hollow-eyed look. His erratic nervous energy fired a considerable creative talent.*

out, Sophie took work as a governess in Felixstowe, about 80 miles away on the east coast. Letters flowed between them, full of sun and an almost pagan love. They exchanged ideas about life and art, and consoled each other.

During this period of correspondence they adopted pet names for one another. Henri was Pik, Pikus, or Pipik; and Sophie was "beloved little Mamus," "adored Mamuska," Zosik, or Sisik. Largely at Henri's insistence, Sophie gave up her work as a governess and came back to London, where they lived in a series of damp, dilapidated houses. They were always hungry. Sophie bought and cooked the whole week's food on Monday—meat, potatoes, and herrings— and they ate the same fare cold, stretched with a little bread and milk, until the following Monday. Underfed, gaunt, and subject to powerful fits of emotion, Henri was described by a fellow artist who knew him during this period as,

"probably the dirtiest human being ever known."

Sophie was becoming increasingly tense and neurotic as well. She upset many of the people whom Henri hoped would buy his drawings and sculptures. Both were proud, never admitting to others that they needed money—Henri would give away work rather than sell it—and they both had such volatile tempers that the strain was often impossible to bear.

Both Henri and Sophie suffered from recurring guilt, terrifying moods, and sudden bursts of joy, as evidenced by many of the anecdotes recorded in Sophie's diary. On one occasion, determined to be happy, Henri devoted

Left *Henri's* Maternité *(1913), expressive of his relationship with Sophie. In the trenches in 1914, he made a another "Maternity" statue from the butt-end of a rifle.*

HENRI GAUDIER
(1891–1915)
was born in St. Jean-de-Braye, central France, the son of a carpenter and a descendant of several generations of stonemasons. He studied art (and some business affairs) in Orléans, Bristol, Nuremberg, and Munich. From early 1911 he worked as a sculptor in London, later attracting the patronage of the poet Ezra Pound. One of the first creators of abstract sculptures, he became a member of the Vorticist movement—led by Percy Wyndham Lewis—which aimed to reflect the modern industrial world in art, using angular abstract shapes to give the impression of movement. His most famous works include the sculptures *The Dancer* and *The Embracers*. He was also a fine painter and sketcher. Henri died fighting for France in World War I, on June 5, 1915, at the age of 24.

SOPHIE BRZESKA
(1873–d. ?)
was born near Cracow in Poland, the only daughter in a family of nine children. From the age of 16, she had ambitions to be a writer but had little success. Sophie studied in Cracow, then worked in Paris, Philadelphia, and New York as a poorly paid governess. She was prone to ill health and depression all her life, afflictions that were exacerbated by constant poverty. Before 1910, when she met Henri Gaudier in Paris, she had made many unsuccessful attempts to find a husband. From late 1910 to 1914 she lived mainly in London with Henri. Although increasingly neurotic, she was widely read and loved to discuss art and literature with Henri, with whom she had a platonic and largely maternal relationship. She outlived Henri and died—poor and alone—in a mental institution.

Above Mademoiselle Brzeska, *one of Henri's portraits of Sophie, worked in pastels and completed in 1913, three years after the couple met in Paris.*

many hours one night to modeling a bust of Sophie as she sang folk songs from her childhood. But the next day they quarreled over money, and in anger, Henri damaged the statue while Sophie was out. The next morning, both furious, they destroyed it together. Yet they remained devoted to one another. Driven by raw energy and boundless enthusiasm, Henri would make a hundred rapid drawings during his London life classes, while others finished one. He would capture in a quick sketch a panther's grace or the alertness of deer. His energy brought clarity to his statues.

There is no evidence that Sophie's own work—her attempts at writing—were ever published. Unlike Henri, she was forever refining the same piece,

"her work always in a state of preparation,"

as Henri said. Where he was direct, she was hesitant. Their love, intense but often confused, mirrored this pattern: they were neither brother and sister, nor mother and son, nor lovers in the full sense. During

a separation of several months in 1912, when Sophie was living in the country for the sake of her health, they exchanged many intense letters—including the one extracted here—Henri writing almost every other day. Various passages from this correspondence suggest Henri desired a more physical relationship.

"I kiss my dear Zosik, all over her dear body, and recommend her to the care of the beneficent sun,"

he wrote in one particularly tender passage.

When war broke out in 1914, Henri went to fight for France. He wrote to Sophie saying they should marry when he came home. It crossed with her letter blaming him for the state of her life in England. She did not reply at once to his proposal, and when she did finally compose a letter, she waited to send it, adding afterthoughts. Before it was mailed, she heard that Henri had died during the attack on Neuville St. Vaast on June 5. Theirs was the love of two unconventional and tempestuous spirits, passionate and intense while still remaining chaste. Sophie kept her diary for the next seven years, and died an obscure death in a mental hospital some years later.

Prague, April 25, 1927

Dear soul!

 Believe me, I cannot escape from our two walks. Like a heavy, beautiful dream; in which I am bewitched.

 I know that I'd be consumed in that heat which cannot catch fire. On the paths I'd plant oaks which would endure for centuries; and into their trunks I'd carve the words which I shouted into the air. I don't want them to be lost, I want them to be known.

 To no-one, ever, have I spoken these words with such compulsion, so recklessly: "You, you, Kamila! Look back! Stop!" and I read in your eyes as well that something united us in that gale-force wind and heat of the sun. Perhaps something was fated to give us both unutterable pleasure? Never in my life have I experienced such an intermingling of myself with you. We walked along not even close to one another and yet there was no gap between us. I was just your shadow, for me to be there it needed you. I'd have wished that walk to be without an end; I waited without tiring for the words which you whispered; what would I have done were you my wife? Well, I think of you as if you were my wife. It's a small thing just to think like that, and yet it's as if the rays of a hundred suns were overwhelming me. I think this to myself and I won't stop thinking it.

 Do with this letter, this confession of mine, what you will. Burn it, or don't burn it. It brings me alive. Even thoughts become flesh.

 Keep well.

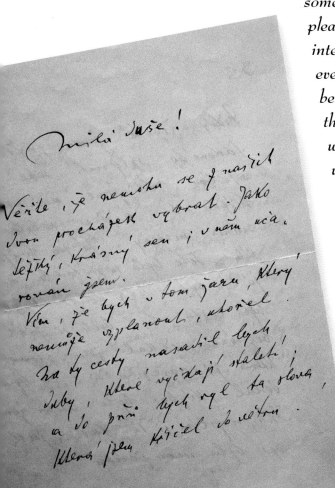

The famous Czech composer Leoš Janáček met Kamila Stösslová in July 1917 at the spa town of Luhačovice, where she was staying with her husband, David Stössel. Janáček was then 63, while Kamila—a woman of striking good looks—was only 25 years old. Kamila became his fantasy lover, his grand passion, and the inspiration for some of his greatest music. She was also an outlet for all his repressed anxieties and hopes. In the last 12 years of his life he wrote her some 700 letters, including the one extracted here, written the year before he died and encapsulating his feelings for her. Kamila, in turn, wrote him only occasional letters, most of which Janáček burned at her request. Her initial cool detachment gradually developed into a warm acceptance of a love she never fully understood.

After his meeting with Kamila, Janáček excitedly told his wife, Zdenka—to whom he had been married for 36 years—about the couple he had just met. In Zdenka's autobiography *My Life* (1935) she recorded that he said at the time,

> "...they really love one another."

Zdenka was at first pleased with his new friendship and saw it as a safe distraction for her husband. Kamila—a happily married woman, and mother of two boys—posed no threat to her. Besides, when Zdenka met her in August, she liked her. In her autobiography, she recalled:

> "I thought she was quite nice: young, cheerful, one could have a really good talk with her, she was always laughing."

She felt the couple

> "brought action and laughter into our sad quietness."

David Stössel was also pleased by the new friendship, proud to have the famous composer as a family friend.

In the beginning of their friendship, Leoš and Kamila met occasionally and exchanged letters from their homes at opposite ends of the country. The artlessness in Kamila that made Zdenka smile more and more entranced Janáček. She did not try to attract him, nor did she want to. She knew that even their "innocent friendship" might upset Zdenka. By September 30, 1922, Janáček's feelings for Kamila had intensified. He wrote:

> "I'm so glad that we've said openly to one another that we're friends. It's an ideal friendship and I'm so glad that it's so pure and elevated above everything bad....You don't know how sad it would be for me without you—although sometimes I don't see you for years!"

Right *Family friends: Leoš Janáček (far right) next to his wife Zdenka, and Kamila Stösslová (far left) with her husband David, in Písek in 1925. Although Kamila allowed Janáček his fantasy, she remained married to her husband.*

Below *The original score of Janáček's Second String Quartet, "Intimate Pages." Inspired by his love of Kamila, he wrote the work in just 20 days.*

In June 1924, after staying with the Stössels for what he described as

"three beautiful days without a shadow,"

Janáček wrote to Kamila:

"And do you know what else makes me glad? That once again I saw your raven-black hair, all loose, your bare foot: and you are beautiful, wonderfully beautiful....And your eye has a strange depth, it's so deep that it doesn't shine. But it's more attractive: as if it wanted to embrace....Kamila if it weren't for you I wouldn't want to live. It's just an alliance of our souls which binds us."

The following month, on July 9, Kamila replied to his extravagant prose. Poorly educated, she was not used to expressing herself in writing, and her spelling and punctuation often went awry. She wrote matter-of-factly, with none of Janáček's mystical quality. Having long resisted being drawn into a relationship that existed largely in Janáček's imagination, she finally relented:

"I write a bit sadly but I've read your letters and so I sense that love of yours for me. Where I'm sorry is if someone is suffering....So be terribly cheerful because that's what I wish. For it's beautiful that you have these memories of me that's enough for you....I never thought I'd correspond with some man and I resisted even you....But fate wanted otherwise so we'll now leave everything to fate. It's better that you're so old now, if you were young my husband would never permit this...."

Above *The cover of the score of Janáček's opera Kát'a Kabanová, drawn by Vladimir Hrska, designer of the first production. Kát'a, the female lead, was firmly associated in Janáček's mind with Kamila.*

Right *Janáček and Kamila first met in July 1917 in the fashionable spa town of Luhačovice, where they were staying with their spouses. They would certainly have strolled together along the promenade, seen here in a watercolor by Jaroslav Setelik, c.1918–20.*

Janáček was quite clear about the limits beyond which they could not go. He wrote in reply:

> "But I know, don't I, that I'll never have you. Would I pluck that flower, that family happiness of yours, would I make free with my respect for you whom I honor like no other woman on earth?....So I dream about you and I know that you're the unattainable sky."

In March 1927 Zdenka suggested that Janáček should stay with the Stössels while their own house was being painted. After the few days spent with them, he wrote Kamila the passionate letter printed here, which shows their "affair" at its height. Many more letters passed between them and they met occasionally, but not until August 1927 did they finally kiss. At times there was a strong strand of delusion in Janáček's passion. He thought of Kamila as his "wife," and even imagined that she was pregnant, though in fact she was just putting on weight as she got older. Inspired by Kamila, Janáček—by then in his mid-seventies—wrote some of his most powerful music, including his famous *Second String Quartet*. He inscribed it first "Love Letters," and then "Intimate Pages." As Janáček wrote to her:

> "In every work of mine there is at least a shadow of your soul…"

and, capturing something of the beauty he saw in her,

> "every note will be your dark eye."

Kamila, baffled by his feelings, was concerned not to hurt Zdenka. On March 5, 1928, she wrote to him:

> "It pains me how you wrote that your wife is suffering on my account perhaps you could devote a little love toward her too….I make no claims on anything. But she's your wife and she has claims on everything…"

Leoš Janáček did, at least, know what it meant to be in love. On March 28, 1928, a few months before his death, he wrote to Kamila:

> "Well, love is a wizard. Submit to it faithfully and it gives a person joy. It intoxicates, it envelops, it isolates. It creates fragrance in the air, ardor from coldness, it beautifies everything around it."

It was Kamila—his great love and muse—and not his wife, who was with him when he died.

Above *Janáček's cottage in Hukvaldy, his birthplace. At some point it was sold and passed out of the family, but Janáček bought it back in 1921, and in 1928 added the upstairs room for Kamila to use when she came to visit him there.*

❧ *The Lovers* ❧

LEOŠ JANÁČEK (1854–1928) was born in Hukvaldy, Moravia, formerly part of the Austrian Empire (now in the Czech Republic). He studied music in Prague, Leipzig, and Vienna. In 1881 he founded the Brno Organ School, which he directed for 40 years. After the creation of Czechoslovakia in 1918, he fought hard for the school to be turned into a conservatory financed by the state. Janáček's deep interest in Moravian folk music and speech inflection influenced many of his later operas and much of his instrumental music. His best-known works are the operas *Jenůfa* (1904), *Kát'a Kabanová* (1921), *The Cunning Little Vixen* (1924), *The Makropoulos Case* (1926), and *From the House of the Dead* (1930). He also wrote song cycles and choral works. In 1881 he married 15-year-old Zdenka Schulz. They had two children, both short-lived: Olga (1883–1903) and Vladimir (1890–92).The marriage lasted—if in name only —until Janáček's death in 1928.

KAMILA STÖSSLOVÁ (NÉE NEUMANNOVÁ) (1891–1935) was born in Putim near Písek, Bohemia, of Jewish parents. In May 1912 she married an antiques dealer, David Stössel, and had two sons by him, Rudolph (b. 1913) and Otto (b. 1916). In 1917, while visiting the spa town of Luhačovice with her husband, she met the 63-year-old composer Leoš Janáček, who fell passionately in love with her. She became the inspiration for some of his greatest music, including the *Second String Quartet*, and the model for the female leads in three of his operas. Kamila was with Janáček when he died in 1928. Seven years later she died of cancer, at age 43.

Frida Kahlo to Diego Rivera

July 23, 1935

[I know now that] all these letters, liaisons with petticoats, lady teachers of "English," gypsy models, assistants with "good intentions," "plenipotentiary emissaries from distant places," only represent flirtations, and that at bottom you and I love each other dearly, and thus go through adventures without number, beatings on doors, imprecations, insults, international claims—yet we will always love each other....

All these things have been repeated throughout the seven years that we have lived together, and all the rages I have gone through have served only to make me understand in the end that I love you more than my own skin, and that, though you may not love me in the same way, still you love me somewhat. Isn't that so?... I shall always hope that that continues, and with that I am content.

Above *Frida and her husband Diego with one of their pet monkeys—Caimito de Guayabal ("guava-patch fruit")— which he gave her as a present.*

Right *Frida and Diego's house in the Mexico City suburb of San Angel, where they moved in 1933. The building symbolized their turbulent relationship: two separate houses linked at roof level by a bridge.*

On July 23, 1935, from her hotel in New York City, the Mexican artist Frida Kahlo wrote to her husband, the great mural painter, Diego Rivera. The letter, extracted here, was one of the most direct and realistic letters of her life, penned during one of the many separations that peppered their tempestuous marriage. What drove her away this time was her discovery that Rivera had had an affair with her younger sister, Christina. Frida's resentment waned, however. In its wake, she seems to have decided that there was a context of mutual love in which she could understand, or at least forgive, his frequent philandering.

In appearance, Frida and Diego made an unlikely couple: she, physically petite and darkly beautiful; he, corpulent and ugly. Together, their lives were pure theater: written about in the press and watched with fascination by the bohemian art circles of the time.

Frida's deep obsession with Rivera began at an early age. According to one account, the 15-year-old Frida first saw him—then 36 years old, a Communist, and a world-famous artist—when he was painting murals at her preparatory school in the heart of Mexico City. She told startled friends,

> *"My ambition is to have a child by Diego Rivera. And I'm going to tell him so some day."*

By the time she met Rivera on more adult terms, she was 21 and a painter herself. He encouraged her art, but courted her as well, attracted by her quick intelligence, her hatred of bourgeois convention, and her direct, often ironic, sense of humor. While painting Frida's portrait as a Communist militant for a mural, he joked:

> *"You have a dog face"*

to which Frida lovingly retorted:

> *"And you have the face of a frog!"*

Right In her 1943 Self-Portrait as a Tehuana (Diego in my Thoughts), *Frida revealed both a love of Mexican folk costume and, more poignantly, an obsessive longing for Rivera.*

In 1929 Frida and Diego married, she for the first time, he for the third. She could not fulfill her adolescent dream of bearing him a child, because of injuries sustained in a bus accident that occurred when she was 18. But Frida was a loyal wife, defending him from critics, worrying about his health, and traveling with him wherever commissions took him, whether to San Francisco, Detroit, or New York.

Frida knew from the outset that Diego could not be possessed, that art was his first passion, followed by Mexico, Marxism, and "the people." She wrote:

> *"Diego is beyond all limited and precise personal relations. He does not have friends, he has allies: he is very affectionate, but he never surrenders himself."*

To some extent this suited Frida, allowing her to forge her own career and social life. The home

Rivera built for them reflected their relationship: two houses, linked by a bridge. Frida had lovers (male and female), including such luminaries as the sculptor, Isamu Noguchi, and Leon Trotsky. The men she kept secret to avoid Rivera's murderous jealousy.

By the midsummer of 1939, ten years after their marriage and after a trip to Paris where Frida was hailed by the Surrealists, she and Rivera had begun divorce proceedings. Frida wrote:

> *"I see him very often but he doesn't want to live in the same house with me anymore because he likes to be alone....Well anyway I take care of him the best I can from the distance...and I will love him all my life even if he wouldn't want me to."*

Their divorce lasted about a year. Neither could stand the separation. Rivera told a friend,

> *"I'm going to marry her because she really needs me."*

Right *Frida's 1949 painting* The Love Embrace of the Universe, the Earth (Mexico), Diego, Me and Señor Xolotl *is rich in private symbolism. In the middle, Frida holds Diego in the pose of the Madonna and Child, reflecting her strong maternal feelings for Rivera. (Señor Xolotl was the name of their dog.)*

Left *A love note from Frida to Diego written on a hospital bag meant for a patient's valuables.*

But Rivera also needed Frida, and was prepared to accept several key conditions that she laid down for remarriage, among them that she would support herself financially from her painting, and that there would be no lovemaking. Rivera explained that,

> *"with the images of all my other women flashing through her mind...a psychological barrier would spring up as soon as I made advances."*

Married to each other for the second time in December 1940, their lives continued in much the same vein as before. They took pride in each other's work, fought, reconciled, and pursued others. Throughout, Rivera remained central to Frida's life. In an entry in her journal in the late 1940's she wrote:

> *"Diego: Nothing is comparable to your hands and nothing is equal to the gold-green of your eyes....My fingertips touch your blood."*

When his infidelities became too much, she would adopt a maternal role, grumbling about his untidiness,

> *"Oh that boy, already he has spoiled his shirt,"*

or bathing and cleaning him as if he were a child.

By the late 1940's, Frida and Rivera were Olympian figures in the Mexican art world. Perhaps Frida's greatest triumph was her first solo exhibition in Mexico City, in 1953. She was so ill that she had to be carried into the gallery on a stretcher and laid on a four-poster bed. Diego supported her as much as he could through her illness, putting up with her unpredictable behavior. She never lost her desire for him and confided to a friend shortly before her death:

> *"I only want three things in life: to live with Diego, to continue painting and to belong to the Communist party."*

Such hopes were short-lived. After a bout of pneumonia, Frida died two weeks later on July 13, 1954.

❧ *The Lovers* ❧

FRIDA KAHLO
(1907–54)
was born in Mexico City, the third daughter of a devout Mexican woman of Spanish and Indian descent, and of a Jewish German-born photographer, Guillermo Kahlo. Her earliest years coincided with the bloody Mexican Revolution. At 18, a bus accident left her with lifelong physical and mental pain. She began painting in 1926 while recuperating. Frida married Rivera in 1929, divorced him in 1939, and remarried him a year later. In the 1940's her career grew to rival that of her husband. Much of her work, especially the many self-portraits—such as *Self-Portrait with Cropped Hair* (1940)—are full of symbolism reflecting obsessions with pain, fertility, desolation, and—above all—with Rivera himself.

DIEGO RIVERA
(1886–1957)
was a child prodigy who went to Mexico's national art school, the San Carlos Academy, when he was just 10 years old. In 1907, at age 20, he was awarded a scholarship to study in Europe. There he befriended, and was influenced by, the pioneer Cubists, including Picasso. He was soon taken, though, by the idea of a monumental public art that would inspire ordinary people, draw on the rich culture of Mexico, and convey the revolutionary Marxist gospel. Encouraged by the Socialist Mexican government to revive fresco painting, Rivera became a master mural painter. His major works included frescoes for the Ministry of Education, the National Agricultural School at Chapingo, and the Detroit Institute of Arts.

Star-crossed Lovers

"... It's a very mysterious thing,

that electric thing that happens,

and then the agony that can follow.

The troubadours celebrate the agony

of the love, the sickness the

doctors cannot cure, the wound....

The wound is the wound of my passion

and the agony of my love for this creature.

The only one who can heal me

is the one who delivered the blow."

JOSEPH CAMPBELL,
The Power of Myth

Heloise to Abelard

Mid–12th Century

You know, beloved, as the whole world knows, how much I have lost in you, how at one wretched stroke of fortune that supreme act of flagrant treachery robbed me of my very self in robbing me of you; and how my sorrow for my loss is nothing compared with what I feel for the manner in which I lost you. You are the sole cause of my sorrow, and you alone can grant me the grace of consolation. You alone have the power to make me sad, to bring me happiness or comfort. God knows I never sought anything in you except yourself; I wanted simply you, nothing of yours.

I looked for no marriage-bond, no marriage portion, and it was not my own pleasures and wishes I sought to gratify, as you well know, but yours. The name of wife may seem more sacred or more binding, but sweeter to me will always be the word mistress, or, if you will permit me, that of concubine or whore.

Remember, I implore you, what I have done, and think how much you owe me. While I enjoyed with you the pleasures of the flesh, many were uncertain whether I was prompted by love or lust; but now the end is proof of the beginning. I have finally denied myself every pleasure in obedience to your will, kept nothing of myself except to prove that now, even more, I am yours.

And so, in the name of God to whom you have dedicated yourself, I beg you to restore your presence to me in the way you can—by writing me some word of comfort, so that in this at least I may find increased strength and readiness to serve God. I beg you, think what you owe me, give ear to my pleas, and I will finish a long letter with a brief ending; farewell, my only love.

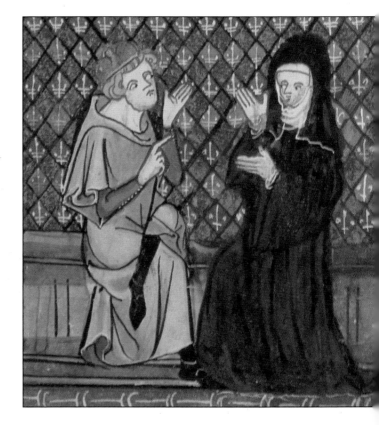

Right *A 14th-century illumination of Abelard and Heloise in religious habits, from the manuscript of* Le Roman de la Rose, *a popular love poem that preserved the lovers' story for posterity.*

The French poet Lamartine said that one does not tell the 12th-century story of Heloise and Abelard, one sings it. It is a story of passion, revenge, steadfastness, and deep spirituality. Our knowledge of this very private love affair between a monk and a nun is based on their correspondence after many years of silence, triggered when Peter Abelard wrote a letter to console a troubled friend, telling the friend of his own calamitous life. Your problems, he claimed, are nothing compared with what I have suffered, yet God can turn the worst situations to serve His own good. By chance, Heloise saw what Abelard had written, and in the letter extracted here, asked why he did not write to console her as well. The story was hers too, and he had not told it as it really was.

Peter Abelard was born in 1079 in Brittany. Determined to study philosophy, he became a wandering scholar, seeking out teachers wherever he went. Sharp, self-confident, bristling with new ideas and methods, he soon clashed with the teachers he met and began to give classes of his own. Wherever he went, students crowded around to learn from him. In 1115, at the age of 36, his achievements were recognized when he was appointed Master at the great school of Notre Dame in Paris.

One of the canons of Notre Dame cathedral, Fulbert, had an attractive teenage niece named Heloise. She was an orphan who lived in his care and Fulbert took great pride in her. Because she was highly intelligent, he made a bargain with the new scholar of philosophy. Abelard could live at their house in exchange for giving Heloise private lessons. It was, Abelard wrote,

> "giving a newborn lamb into the care of a hungry wolf."

For Abelard, a cleric in minor orders, the young Heloise was irresistible. In spite of his moral scruples and religious vows, he seduced her and soon became obsessed with Heloise. Neglecting his studies of philosophy, he turned poet, and the songs that he wrote for her were sung throughout the streets of Paris. Heloise, in turn, abandoned herself to her growing love for her tutor, Abelard.

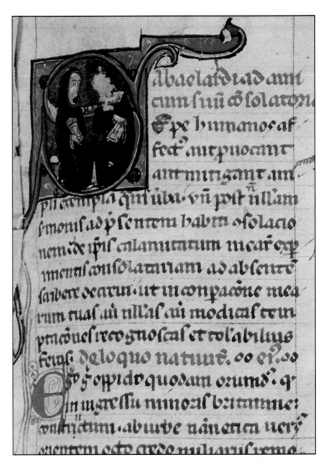

Above *An illuminated manuscript copy of Abelard's account of his story, the* Historia Calamitatum. *This copy belonged to the Italian sonneteer, Francesco Petrarch (1304-74). The illustration of the two lovers in the top left-hand corner has been defaced.*

In 1118 she gave birth to a baby boy. Her uncle Fulbert was enraged, and in an effort to atone, Abelard said that he would marry Heloise—providing that it could be kept secret so as not to damage his career. It was not impossible for teachers of philosophy to marry, but it was unusual. Fulbert agreed to the arrangement, but Heloise would have nothing to do with it. She did not want Abelard to take on the burdens of marriage or to distract himself from study. Heloise was willing to make the sacrifice of loneliness and social disgrace for the sake of love, but Abelard insisted they marry. Eventually they were married in secret. Abelard went on teaching, and Heloise stayed at home with her uncle, who, in his anger, told people what had really happened. To save

Heloise from further embarrassment, Abelard took her to the community of nuns at the convent at Argenteuil, outside Paris. Fulbert, thinking that Abelard was trying to abandon responsibility for his niece, looked for revenge by hiring some thugs to assault the young scholar. They brutally castrated him. Shamed and unable to face the world, Abelard sought refuge in the monastery of St. Denis.

The lovers, now monk and nun, began to reconstruct their separate lives. Heloise made her way toward becoming an abbess. Abelard resumed both teaching and writing, and proved as brilliant and controversial as ever. Two years later he founded his own religious community, the Paraclete—the Comforter—near Troyes, and began to teach there. Then, in 1125 he was elected abbot of a remote, unruly monastery in his native Brittany, and left the order he had founded. Five years later, he gave the convent of the Paraclete to Heloise and her community. It was soon after this, when his life was endangered by scheming Breton monks, that he wrote to console a troubled friend, reliving events from 16 years before. Seducing Heloise had brought disaster on the lovers, he explained, but out of disaster, God had brought a greater good. They both loved God and had been reconciled to following his will.

When Heloise, entirely by chance, saw his account of their life together—it is not known how it came into her hands—she wrote to Abelard. Perhaps he had willingly embraced a life of penance, she told him, but she had not. Her passionate desires remained painfully unabated. She felt that consolation could come only from Abelard, not from God. She explained in her letter,

> *"I have as yet done nothing for Him. I should certainly groan about what I have done, but I sigh rather over what I have lost."*

In the same letter, she asked Abelard how she could ever learn to be satisfied with the religious life of a nun. Once more Abelard reviewed their past. Heloise had been the greater lover. He had tried to possess her, forcing first marriage and then convent life on her. But her love, though not possessive, was nevertheless misdirected. Earthly love, he argued, pales in the light of the love of God. That was where they must find the fullness of their own love, as man and woman, abbot and abbess, husband and wife. Catastrophe, he explained to her, had saved them for a higher love:

> *"See then my beloved, see how with the dragnets of his mercy the Lord has fished us up from the depths of the dangerous sea."*

Was Heloise persuaded? It seems that she was at least reconciled to the inevitable. From "a grieving heart" she asked Abelard to do something that she knew would make use of his talents as a religious philosopher. She asked him to set down guidelines for herself and her nuns to live by. In considering convent life, Abelard was forced to picture Heloise's daily existence. At least she knew that for a period of time she was always in his thoughts.

In life, they never came together again; but in death they lay together at the convent of the Paraclete, as Abelard had wished. Legend claims that when Heloise was buried in 1164, 22 years after Abelard, he reached out from the grave to embrace her.

Left *A medieval abbess and her pupil in animated discussion, surrounded by a group of ladies (from* Poems of Charles Duke of Orleans and other works by the same Hand, *c. 1500). After her separation from Abelard, Heloise lived out her life as an abbess.*

The
❧ Lovers ❧

HELOISE
(c.1098–1164)

was raised by her uncle Fulbert and educated at the convent at Argenteuil. When she was about 17 she had a passionate affair with the brilliant theologian and philosopher Peter Abelard, her private tutor. She bore him a son, Astralabe. Soon after, the couple were secretly married, but to protect her reputation and Abelard's career, Heloise agreed to enter the convent at Argenteuil, where she later became abbess. Famous for her intellect and erudition, she wrote and spoke Latin, read Greek, and had an encyclopedic knowledge of the classics and scriptures. In later life she founded several convents, but remained deeply in love with Abelard all her life, and was eventually buried beside him. They now lie in Père Lachaise cemetery in Paris.

PETER ABELARD
(1079–1142)

was one of the leading French philosophers of his time. He is best known for his moving relationship with Heloise, and the barbaric revenge of her uncle Fulbert, who had him castrated. During his monastic life Abelard made notable contributions to the development of teaching methods, to theological inquiry, and to questions of faith and ethics. In *Sic et non* he laid down rules for resolving apparently contradictory biblical texts. He also did important work on the theology of the Trinity and on the philosophical question of whether abstract ideas can be said to exist. An outstanding teacher, he was one of a cluster of scholars whose presence in the city led ultimately to the foundation of the University of Paris. Although his controversial views were officially condemned by the church in 1121 and 1140, he was a man whose deep faith shone through a troubled life.

Left *The tomb of Abelard and Heloise at Père Lachaise cemetery in Paris. Their remains were moved here in the 19th century.*

Catherine of Aragon to Henry VIII of England

January, 1536

My most dear lord, king and husband,
The hour of my death now
approaching, I cannot choose but out of the
love I bear you, advise you of your soul's
health, which you ought to prefer before all
considerations of the world or flesh
whatsoever. For which yet you have cast me
into many calamities, and your self into
many troubles. But I forgive you all; and
pray God to do so likewise. For the rest, I
commend unto you Mary, our daughter,
beseeching you to be a good father to her, as I
have heretofore desired. I must entreat you
also, to respect my maids, and give them in
marriage, which is not much, they being but three; and to all my
other servants a year's pay, besides their due, lest otherwise they
should be unprovided for; lastly, I make this vow, that
mine eyes desire you above all things.
Farewell.

Above *A portrait of the young Catherine of Aragon, painted by M. Sittou (date unknown). She was 23 years old when she married Henry, at age 17, on June 11, 1509.*

Right *The letter (second paragraph) as it appeared in Latin in a medieval history book of 1555,* Anglicae Historiae, *by Polydorus Vergilius.*

Weak and approaching death, Catherine of Aragon, the Spanish princess and former wife of Henry VIII, dictated her last letter to him. She began with a wifely admonition, and ended with a loving plea to see him again,

"mine eyes desire you above all things."

A few hours later she died, according to her chaplain still asking God's pardon for,

"the king her husband, for the wrong he had done her."

Catherine was the youngest daughter of the powerful Spanish rulers, Ferdinand of Aragon and Isabella of Castile, and had an important part to play in Spanish policy. Catherine was to cement an alliance with England by marrying the heir to the throne, Prince Arthur, the elder son of Henry VII. On October 2, 1501, she landed at Plymouth in England, and married Arthur a month later—he was 14 and she 16. Within six months Arthur lay dead in Ludlow Castle, the victim of an epidemic.

Henry VII was reluctant to lose the alliance with Spain and determined not to return Catherine's dowry, so it was decided that she should marry Prince Henry, Arthur's younger brother. He was only 11 years old, and 14 was the minimum legal age for marriage, so Catherine waited, at the mercy of the gossip-ridden English court, while European politics shifted behind the scenes. Through her years of widowhood Prince Henry was one of Catherine's few regular visitors and a genuine affection grew up between them. As Henry VII began to regret the promised marriage and seek other allies, his son began to desire the match for love, not for political advantage. By the time the prince was 17, the couple were still not married. Then, in 1509, just as Catherine was making preparations to return to Spain, the old king died, and young Henry ascended the throne. Exercising his new authority, he married Catherine almost immediately.

"If I were still free, I would choose her for my wife before all others,"

wrote Henry VIII to his father-in-law, Ferdinand.

Early in 1510, Catherine's first pregnancy ended, as did so many in the Tudor age, with a stillborn baby. On January 1, 1511, she gave birth to a baby boy, who died seven weeks later. This pattern repeated itself; in spite of Catherine's many pregnancies, only one child, Mary, survived. The lack of an heir was a constant anxiety, but in all other respects the king and queen seemed an ideal and loving couple. Visiting the English court in 1520, Erasmus wrote:

"What family of citizens offers so clear an example of strict and harmonious wedlock?"

Then in the spring of 1526 Henry became infatuated with Anne Boleyn, one of Catherine's ladies-in-waiting. He had had affairs before, but Anne resisted

Above *Henry VIII, by Hans Holbein the Younger, c. 1538. Henry was extremely vain about his appearance, and asked the artist to make a particular feature of his shapely legs.*

Above *A writing desk belonging to Henry VIII, decorated with his own portrait and heraldic badges (the portcullis and the tudor rose) and those of Catherine (the pomegranate and the fleur-de-lys).*

Henry's advances, insisting on marriage first. Henry had needed the pope's dispensation to marry Catherine, since marriage to a brother's widow was forbidden without special permission. Now Henry argued that his expedient marriage to Catherine had broken God's law. He feared—or said he feared—that he had been punished by God for this transgression through the death of his male children. Through long hours of cross-examination Catherine defended her status, emphasizing her devotion and loyalty,

> *"I love and have loved my lord the king as much as any woman can love a man, but I would not have borne him company as his wife one moment against the voice of my conscience."*

While the pope delayed in Rome, Henry subdued objections in parliament and the English church. However, he seemed reluctant to say anything that attacked Catherine personally. Throughout the legal battles he praised the queen as a lady,

> *"against whom no word could be spoken."*

He continued,

> *"If it be adjudged that the Queen is my lawful wife, nothing will be more pleasant or more acceptable to me....If I were to marry again, I would choose her above all women."*

If, however, the marriage were ruled unlawful,

> *"...then shall I sorrow, parting from so good a lady and loving companion."*

On July 11, 1531, Henry rode out from Windsor to go hunting—Catherine never saw him again. Satisfied with the decisions he had forced from the church in England, Henry married Anne Boleyn in secret. She was crowned queen with full public splendor on June 1, 1533, when she was already six months pregnant. Henry believed that God showed approval through the pregnancy, and confidently expected a son, but Anne gave birth to a baby girl, the future Elizabeth I. Henry was devastated, and a worse blow was to follow. In March 1534, the pope declared Catherine's marriage with Henry still valid. He had left himself no choice but to reject the pope's authority. English statesmen and clerics who refused to accept reform were executed. Catherine, though spared execution, was cut off from all but a few loyal friends and servants. She died on January 7, 1536.

A few months later, Anne was executed for adultery. Within 24 hours, Henry married his third wife, Jane Seymour. His 22-year marriage to Catherine had been based on loyalty and affection. The rapid succession of marriages that followed (divorced, beheaded, died, divorced, beheaded, survived) suggested that Henry never found that stability again.

Below A section of the Westminster Tournament Roll, showing celebrations for the birth of a son to Catherine and Henry in 1511 The queen is in the center of the grandstand, while the king waits to joust. The death of the prince was a fatal blow to the marriage.

Above Henry's unsuccessful petition to the pope, dated 1530, asking for the annulment of his marriage to Catherine. His case was supported by the English bishops who signed in agreement.

❦ *The Lovers* ❦

CATHERINE OF ARAGON
(1485–1536)
was the youngest daughter of the Spanish monarchs Ferdinand of Aragon and Isabella of Castile. From an early age she was destined to strengthen Spain's alliance with England by marrying the heir to the throne. Widowed by Prince Arthur after only six months, she later married his younger brother, Henry, in what was both a political and a love match. Though she was a firm favorite with the English people, her reign as queen was blighted by Henry VIII's anxiety over the succession to the throne. Although the couple had one surviving female child, all their male offspring died in infancy. Catherine was a devout Catholic and relied on the pope to protect her position, but in his anxiety to produce a son Henry renounced the Catholic Church by divorcing her in a dramatic battle of Church and State that ushered in the English Reformation.

HENRY VIII OF ENGLAND
(1491–1547)
was one of the most powerful of England's kings. He ascended the throne in 1509 and consolidated power in both Church and State in his own person, renouncing papal supremacy, proclaiming himself head of the church, and dissolving the monasteries. He is at least as well remembered for his succession of wives, six in all. The first, Catherine of Aragon, he divorced. The second, Anne Boleyn, he had beheaded for adultery. Jane Seymour, his third wife, died in childbirth in 1537. Anne of Cleves he divorced, and the fifth wife, Catherine Howard, he had beheaded in 1542. The following year he married Catherine Parr, who outlived him. Henry fathered three English sovereigns, the boy-king Edward VI, Mary I (known as "Bloody Mary"), and Elizabeth I. His reign radically reshaped English society and established Protestantism as the state religion.

Robert Emmet to Sarah Curran

September, 1803

My dearest Love,

 I don't know how to write to you. I never felt so oppressed in my life as at the cruel injury I have done you. I was seized and searched with a pistol over me before I could destroy your letters. They have been compared with those found before. I was threatened with having them brought forward against me in Court. I offered to plead guilty if they would suppress them. This was refused. My love, can you forgive me?

 I wanted to know whether anything had been done respecting the person who wrote the letters, for I feared you might have been arrested. They refused to tell me for a long time. When I found, however, that this was not the case, I began to think that they only meant to alarm me; but their refusal has only come this moment, and my fears are renewed. Not that they can do anything to you even if they would be base enough to attempt it, for they can have no proof who wrote them, nor did I let your name escape me once. But I fear they may suspect from the stile [style], and from the hair, for they took the stock [Emmet's cravat into which Sarah had sewn a lock of her hair] from me, and I have not been able to get it back from them, and that they may think of bringing you forward.

 I have written to your father to come to me tomorrow. Had you not better speak to himself tonight? Destroy my letters that there may be nothing against yourself, and deny having any knowledge of me further than seeing me once or twice. For God's sake, write to me by the bearer one line to tell me how you are in spirits.

 I have no anxiety, no care, about myself; but I am terribly oppressed about you. My dearest love, I would with joy lay down my life, but ought I to do more? Do not be alarmed; they may try to frighten you; but they cannot do more. God bless you, my dearest love.

 I must send this off at once; I have written it in the dark. My dearest Sarah, forgive me.

Left A miniature portrait of Robert Emmet in the style of J. Comerford.

On September 8, 1803, Irish patriot Robert Emmet, age 25, wrote this letter from his cell in Kilmainham jail, Dublin. He addressed it to "Miss Sarah Curran, the Priory, Rathfarnham" and handed it to a prison warden, George Dunn, whom he trusted to deliver it. Dunn betrayed him and gave the letter to the government authorities, an action that nearly cost Sarah her life.

Emmet, the son of a Dublin doctor, joined the United Irishmen, a mainly Protestant militia opposed to British rule, while a student at Trinity College, Dublin. In 1798 the militia made plans with the post-revolutionary French government to expel the British forces and establish an independent Ireland. Poor organization defeated them, however, and for a while Emmet went into hiding in France, where he failed to secure Napoleon's support.

Returning to Ireland in October 1802, Emmet soon emerged as the leader of the United Irishmen in Dublin. Plans were made to stage a major uprising

Above *Sarah Curran, from a portrait painted by Edward Corballis in 1802, the year before Robert was executed.*

Right *A ragged note from Sarah to Robert, written with caution shortly before the uprising of 1803.*

in the fall of 1803. Meanwhile, Emmet made a clear statement defining his political goals in the Proclamation of the Provisional Government:

"*…we war not against property—we are against no religious sect—we war not against past opinions or prejudice—we war against English dominion.*"

How well he knew Sarah before this time is unclear. Sarah's brother, Richard, knew Robert well from Trinity College. Her father, John Curran, a distinguished lawyer, defended various members of the United Irishmen who came to trial after the failed 1798 rebellion. Emmet, in 1802 in a letter to a friend, the Marquise de Fontenay, referred to the "tender ties" he had at home. Once back in Ireland, Robert frequently visited Sarah's family at Rathfarnham, even though Sarah's father did not welcome him. Sarah

Left *An engraving by the Irish artist George Cruikshank showing the murder of Lord Kilwarden by Emmet's followers in 1803. Emmet's plans to seize power from the British authorities failed disastrously when the rebellion turned into a street skirmish.*

and Robert became engaged, but kept it a secret because of her father's disapproval. Sarah was enthusiastic about all Robert's revolutionary plans. Her patriotism, youth, and great charm endeared her to all the members of the activist's circle. Emmet's housekeeper, Anne Devlin —whose father was imprisoned in 1798 for harboring rebels, and who was herself tortured and imprisoned after the unsuccessful uprising of 1803—said when questioned by Dr. R. R. Madden (author of *United Irishmen*) 40 years after the uprising:

> *"You could not see Miss Curran and not help liking her…her look was the mildest, and the softest, and the sweetest look you ever saw."*

Following another coup attempt on July 23, 1803, Emmet again went into hiding. He sent Sarah a message asking her to elope with him to the United States. But the couple never left the country. He was arrested the following month, with unsigned love letters from Sarah in his possession.

The earliest letters were simply copies of poems. But the love letters, partly in coded language, were full of information that could identify her as the writer. Later letters expressed her fear of angering her father, and the latest letter focused completely on her anxiety about Robert's safety:

> *"I passed the house you are in twice this day, but did not see you. If I thought you were in safety, I would be comparatively happy, at least. I cannot help listening to every idle report.…I cannot tell you how uneasy I shall be until I know that you have got this. Let me know immediately. I request you to burn it instantly.…Goodbye my dear friend, but not forever."*

Emmet kept all her letters inside his coat. On August 30, at the questioning after his arrest, he was asked point-blank,

> *"By whom were these letters written that were found upon your person?"*

He succeeded in keeping Sarah's name out of the proceedings, mentioning only

Above *The Priory, Rathfarnham, the Curran family home on the outskirts of Dublin. This was where Robert and Sarah met for the first time, but the disapproval of Sarah's father discouraged Robert from becoming a regular visitor there.*

> *"a delicate and virtuous female."*

He then protested,

> *"I would rather give up my own life than injure another person."*

Nine days later, Emmet wrote the letter extracted here, revealing her name, and on September 9 the Curran house was searched. With British soldiers downstairs, Sarah's sister Amelia only just succeeded in burning Emmet's letters. John Philpot Curran, furious that Sarah had threatened their lives and his career, ordered her out of the house. She took refuge with friends a few hundred miles away in Cork. The authorities made an example of Emmet, condemning him to be hanged, drawn, and quartered. His final speech in court, an inspiration to generations of Irish revolutionaries, is still widely quoted today:

> *"…Let no man write my epitaph…Let my memory be left in oblivion and my tomb remain uninscribed until other times and other men can do justice to my character. When my country takes her place among the nations of the earth, then, and not till then, let my epitaph be written. I have done."*

He had not quite done. In a letter to Sarah's brother Richard, he wrote:

"I have injured the happiness of a sister that you love….Oh Richard! I have no excuse to offer, but that I meant the reverse; I intended as much happiness for Sarah as the most ardent lover could have given her. I never did tell you how much I idolised her…."

After Emmet's death, abandoned by her family and living with friends in Cork, at the southeastern tip of the country, she met a soldier named Robert Sturgeon who offered her marriage and a home. They moved to Sicily, but she never fully recovered from her grief. Her story inspired the Irish poet, Thomas Moore, to write a sentimental ballad that ensured her a place in popular Irish culture:

*"She is far from the land where her young
  hero sleeps,
And lovers around her are sighing,
But coldly she turns from their gaze, and weeps,
For her heart in his grave is lying."*

Below *An engraving by George Cruikshank of the trial of Robert Emmet in 1803. For political reasons the British government was eager to publicize Emmet's anti-French feeling, indicated here, but friends of Emmet in the courtroom deny that he made this statement.*

❦ *The Lovers* ❦

ROBERT EMMET
(1778–1803)
was born in Dublin, the youngest of four surviving children born to Dr. Robert Emmet, physician to the lord lieutenant, and his wife Elizabeth. Robert entered Trinity College, Dublin in 1793 where he joined the Society of United Irishmen. Their aim was to end Ireland's domination by England. In 1798, following an unsuccessful rebellion, he fled to France where he tried to canvass support for Irish independence. He met Napoleon Bonaparte but doubted if he could rely on his help, and returned to Dublin in 1802 to plan an uprising without the French. On July 23, 1803, Emmet led one hundred followers through the capital, intending to capture Dublin Castle, the seat of British government. The rebels were defeated, and Emmet went into hiding in the hills outside the city. He was eventually arrested, tried, and hanged on September 20, 1803. His grave has never been found.

SARAH CURRAN
(1782–1808)
was the youngest daughter of John Philpot Curran, an eminent Irish lawyer. She met Emmet through her brother Richard, who was a fellow student at Trinity College. Her father considered Emmet unsuitable, and their courtship was conducted through letters and clandestine meetings. When John Philpot Curran discovered that Sarah was secretly engaged, he treated her so harshly that she had to take refuge with friends in Cork, where she met and married Captain Robert Sturgeon in November 1805. They had a child who did not survive infancy, and Sarah died of consumption on May 5, 1808.

John Keats to Fanny Brawne

October 13, 1819

My Dearest Girl

This moment I have set myself to copy some verses out fair. I cannot proceed with any degree of content. I must write you a line or two and see if that will assist in dismissing you from my Mind for ever so short a time. Upon my Soul I can think of nothing else. The time is passed when I had power to advise and warn you against the unpromising morning of my Life. My love has made me selfish. I cannot exist without you. I am forgetful of everything but seeing you again—my Life seems to stop there—I see no further. You have absorb'd me. I have a sensation at the present moment as though I was dissolving—I should be exquisitely miserable without the hope of soon seeing you. I should be afraid to separate myself far from you. My sweet Fanny, will your heart never change? My love, will it? I have no limit now to my love…Your note came in just here. I cannot be happier away from you. 'Tis richer than an Argosy of Pearles. Do not threat me even in jest. I have been astonished that Men could die Martyrs for religion—I have shuddered at it. I shudder no more—I could be martyr'd for my Religion— Love is my religion—I could die for that. I could die for you. My Creed is Love and you are its only tenet. You have ravish'd me away by a Power I cannot resist; and yet I could resist till I saw you; and even since I have seen you I have endeavoured often "to reason against the reasons of my Love." I can do that no more—the pain would be too great. My love is selfish. I cannot breathe without you.

Yours for ever

John Keats

Left *John Keats by Joseph Severn, in 1819. This is a copy, painted for Fanny, of Severn's original miniature. She kept a lock of Keats's hair in the frame of the picture.*

The letters of the poet John Keats to Fanny Brawne are among the most affecting the world has seen. The one printed here was written on October 13, 1819. Just over a year later Keats died from tuberculosis and Fanny began a six-year period of mourning. Unfortunately, in September 1820, the couple destroyed Fanny's letters to him, just before Keats left for Italy in a last bid to regain his health. No one knows why the letters were destroyed; it may have been that neither wished Fanny to be compromised in later life by written evidence of her powerful feelings as a young unmarried woman. They were deeply in love, but well-meaning people around them did not approve of the match.

The couple met in November 1818 in Hampstead (now a district of London). Keats was living with his friend Charles Brown in one half of a large house, Wentworth Place, and their friends Charles Dilke and his wife lived in the other half. Brown rented out his part of the house each summer, and in 1818 Mrs. Brawne and her family were his tenants. Fanny became friends with the Dilkes and continued to visit after the Brawnes had taken another house in Hampstead. Keats met her at Wentworth Place, and in the summer of 1819 they began to sit together in the garden reading poetry. Keats, writing to his brother shortly after the meeting, thought Fanny,

> "beautiful and elegant, graceful, silly, fashionable and strange."

Keats remembered his meeting with Fanny as love at first sight. He would have told her so but thought she disliked him. In a letter to Fanny on July 25, eight months after their first meeting, Keats wrote,

> "the very first week I knew you I wrote myself your vassal; but burnt the Letter as the very next time I saw you I thought you manifested some dislike to me."

Fanny was 18, blue-eyed, fashion-conscious, witty, and fond of dancing and plays. She was given, Keats wrote, to "acting stylishly." She was also very small; Keats was only five feet tall and sensitive about it.

Fanny's widowed mother was anxious that her two daughters should marry well. She did not view Keats, who in the months that followed their meeting seemed to occupy Fanny's thoughts more and more,

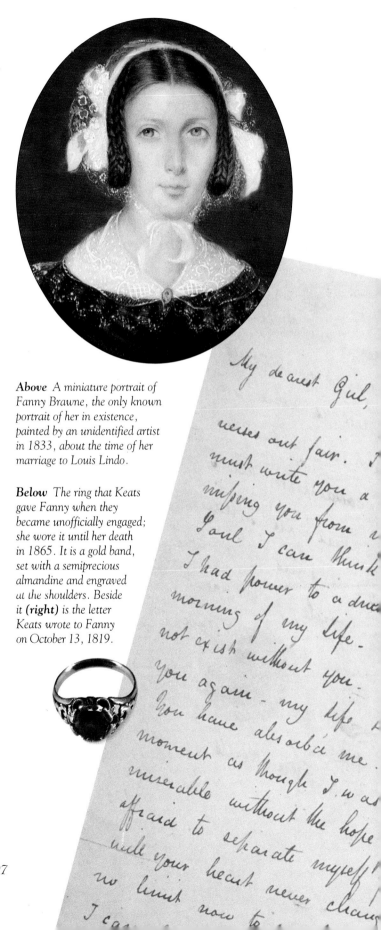

Above A miniature portrait of Fanny Brawne, the only known portrait of her in existence, painted by an unidentified artist in 1833, about the time of her marriage to Louis Lindo.

Below The ring that Keats gave Fanny when they became unofficially engaged; she wore it until her death in 1865. It is a gold band, set with a semiprecious almandine and engraved at the shoulders. Beside it **(right)** is the letter Keats wrote to Fanny on October 13, 1819.

Above Wentworth Place, Hampstead, where Keats and Fanny met. It was built as a two-family residence for the Browns and the Dilkes. Keats stayed there with Charles Brown 1818–20.

as an ideal candidate. In July 1816 he passed the examinations that would allow him to practice as an apothecary-surgeon as soon as he turned 21 years old in October. But before taking up the profession he abandoned the idea and turned his energies to writing poetry full-time. (Earlier works written while he was an apprentice date from 1814.) His first collection of poems, published in 1817, flopped. Fanny's aunts thought the poetry a "mad craze." And Keats's health was not good. In addition, Keats's literary friends disapproved of Fanny: John Reynolds was later to write to Keats's publisher, John Taylor, about the poet's departure for Italy,

> *"Absence from the poor idle Thing of woman-kind, to whom he [Keats] has so unaccountably attached himself, will not be an ill thing."*

In spite of their deep feelings for each other, Keats had no financial prospects that would let him marry. He resolved to concentrate on writing to make money and a name; but to do this, he decided he must move away in order to live cheaply and without distraction. In June he traveled to the Isle of Wight, off the south coast of England, seeking sufficient peace and quiet to write a play. He wrote of his worries in letters to Fanny. His "unguessed fate...spread as a veil" between them. Returning briefly to London to sort out a family problem, he did not allow himself to travel the few extra miles to see Fanny, explaining in a letter to her,

"I love you too much to venture to Hampstead. I feel it is not paying a visit, but venturing into a fire." But on October 10 he saw her again and was overwhelmed. Three days later he wrote the letter printed here, and moved back to Wentworth Place.

The winter of 1819–20 was hard. On February 3, 1820, Keats came home from London, feverish and desperately ill. He went to bed, coughed, and saw blood on the sheet. Charles Brown brought a candle. Together they looked at the blood. Keats said,

"I know the color of that blood; it is arterial blood…. That drop of blood is my death warrant."

That night he suffered a second huge hemorrhage. Absolute rest was necessary to postpone death. Excitement could kill him, so Fanny communicated by notes and small gifts, a vision beyond the window, a visitor who could not stay. Poignantly he wrote,

"I shall follow you with my eyes over the Heath."

As the disease took deeper hold, his moods became more extreme. He worried about Fanny.

"Do not I see a heart naturally furnished with wings imprison itself with me?"

When she was away he felt jealous, but his jealousies were "agonies of love."

"I am sickened at the brute world which you are smiling with."

Cutting short a brief, chaotic stay with his friend, the poet and essayist Leigh Hunt, in nearby Mortimer Terrace, he walked back to Hampstead, arriving exhausted and in tears. Mrs. Brawne took him in, and for his last month in England, she and Fanny nursed him in their home and helped him prepare to go to Italy, where warm skies and dry air might save

❧ The Lovers ❧

JOHN KEATS
(1795–1821)
was a leading figure in the 19th century Romantic movement. In his short career he was a prolific writer of both poetry and letters, the latter to family, friends, and his adored Fanny Brawne. In both he expressed—in the words of Matthew Arnold—a profound "intellectual and spiritual passion" for beauty. His early training was in medicine, but after 1817 he dedicated himself entirely to poetry. In 1818 his first long poem, *Endymion*, was published. During 1819 and 1820 he wrote some of his best-known poems, including *Ode to a Nightingale* and *Ode on a Grecian Urn*, the epic poem *Hyperion*, and the richly evocative *Eve of St. Agnes*, all published in a single volume in 1820. He had two brothers, George and Tom, and a sister, Fanny, to whom he was devoted. Keats died of tuberculosis in Rome on February 23, 1821, at the age of 25. He is buried there in the Protestant Cemetery.

FANNY BRAWNE
(1800–65)
was the eldest of the widowed Mrs. Brawne's three children (she had a brother, Samuel, and sister, Margaret). The family was relatively poor and from humble origins. Fanny's father, like Keats's, had been a stablekeeper. He died of consumption when Fanny was 10. Fanny first met Keats in 1818. Her own interests included historical costume, the latest fashions in clothes, and learning to speak and read French and German. After Keats's death she was in mourning for six years. In 1833 she married Louis Lindo, by whom she had three children. She died at the age of 65.

him. With death on the horizon, the love between Keats and Fanny was at its most powerful, enough to "occupy the widest heart" as Keats had written.

During the voyage to Italy, he wrote to Brown,

"The thought of leaving Miss Brawne is beyond everything horrible….Some of the phrases she was in the habit of using during my last nursing at Wentworth Place ring in my ears…"

Throughout his last days, he held a large white carnelian, a precious stone, that Fanny had given him to cool his fever. On February 23, 1821, Keats died, in the arms of his painter-friend, Joseph Severn. Unopened letters, one from Fanny and one from his sister, were buried with him.

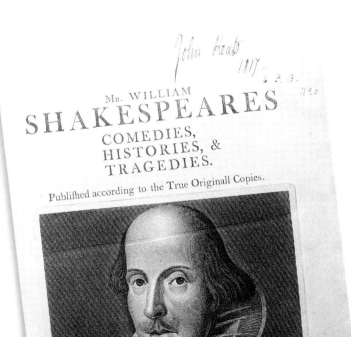

Left and below *Fanny's copy of the works of Shakespeare, inscribed in Keats' handwriting "To F. B." Beside it is a lock of Fanny's hair.*

Mr. WILLIAM
SHAKESPEARES
COMEDIES,
HISTORIES, &
TRAGEDIES.
Publifhed according to the True Originall Copies.

Peter Withers to his wife, Mary Ann

April 1831

My Dear Wife …

We [h]ears we shall get our freedom in that Country, but if I gets my freedom even so i am shure I shall Never be happy except I can have the Pleshur of ending my days with you and my dear Children, for I dont think a man ever loved a woman so well as I love you.

My Dear I hope you will go to the gentlemen for they to pay your Passage over to me when I send for you. How happy I shall be to eare that you are a-coming after me….Do you think I shall sent for you except i can get a Cumfortable place for you, do you think that I wants to get you into Troble, do you think as I want to punish my dear Children? No my dear but if I can get a cumfortable place should you not like to follow your dear Husband who Lovs you so dear?

Right *The "prison hulk" York in Portsmouth harbor, where Peter Withers was detained before the ship H.M.S. Proteus arrived to transport him to Australia.*

In January 1831 a 23-year-old shoemaker, Peter Withers, was sentenced to death. He had taken part in a riot by farm laborers the previous November in the little village of Rockley in Wiltshire, in southern England. During the commotion, Withers had injured a special constable. When the verdict was announced, a local newspaper, *The Dorset County Chronicle*, reported that the prisoners and their grief-stricken families broke down

Above *Farm laborers, c. 1830, threshing wheat by hand. Until the introduction of machines, many country folk like Withers were taken on part-time to do this, providing them with invaluable extra income.*

and wept. Even the judges cried. A petition for a more lenient sentence brought a reprieve, however, and Withers's sentence was commuted to transportation for life to the Australian penal colonies. His offense was recorded as "cutting and maiming." Peter and his fellow convicts were initially kept aboard a rotting "prison hulk"—an old ship used as a temporary place

of detention—in Portsmouth harbor, before the convict ship H.M.S. *Proteus* arrived to take them away. It was from the *Proteus* that Peter wrote the letter extracted here to his young wife, Mary Ann.

Peter's was the fate of many farmworkers in the early 1830's who, faced with unemployment and starvation for both themselves and their families, spontaneously rioted, village by village, all across southern England. They smashed the threshing machines, set fire to hayricks in the fields, and delivered threatening letters to oppressive landlords in the fictitious name of "Captain Swing." Such a reaction was predicted some years before in 1826 by the politician William Cobbett, who reported:

"This is the worst used labouring people upon the face of the earth. Dogs, hogs and horses are treated with more civility…there must be an end to it…and that end will be dreadful."

Although transportation was a severe punishment, it turned out to be a reprieve from the horrors of rural England. For many men and women it meant the chance of a new beginning on the other side of the world. But for Peter and Mary Ann it meant a sudden painful separation after only two brief years of marriage. Mary Ann was faced with the grim prospect of no income and a family of two

Above *An 1809 watercolor of Ramsbury church, as it would have been when Peter and Mary Ann were married there in 1828, just two years before their separation.*

Right *The certificate of marriage of Peter and Mary Ann. Peter signed his name in full, but Mary Ann—like the two witnesses, James Sweeper and Eliza Cruse—had not learned to write, and so marked her name with an "X."*

children to support or—were she to join him—the rigors of the longest sea voyage in the world.

Before the ship *Proteus* sailed, Peter wrote a letter to Mary Ann full of grief at the thought of their separation and the harsh fate that had befallen them:

> *"My Dear wife believe me my Hark [heart] is almost broken to think I must lave you behind. O my dear what shall I do i am all Most destracted at the thoughts of parting from you whom I do love so dear. Believe me My Dear it Cuts me even to the hart and my dear Wife there is a ship Come into Portsmouth harber to take us to New Southweals."*

Mary was fortunate to receive such a touching testimonial of her husband's love—a rare artifact of his time and place. Few of the men sailing with Withers could write more than their own names. When Peter and Mary Ann (née Hobbs) married on October 28, 1828, Peter was the only person present, apart from the minister, who could write his name on the certificate.

In his letter, Peter urged Mary Ann to try to raise passage money by going "to the gentlemen": clergymen, the local magistrate, shop owners, landlords, or

Above *A painting of the Wiltshire yeomanry confronting rioters in November 1830, after they had destroyed three threshing machines that threatened to take away their winter employment. The man at far right is armed, as Withers was, with a blacksmith's hammer.*

Below *The identification details—brown hair, gray eyes, and a round face—of Peter Withers, as recorded by the officials in Tasmania, where Withers was transported. (Fingerprints are the modern equivalent.)*

anyone else who might help sponsor her. Her only other hope lay with the government. Technically, a wife could follow a transported husband once he established himself in the colony. But such cases were rare—for most victims of the system, transportation meant a lifetime's separation from their loved ones and family. Peter tried to reassure her:

"It is about 4 months sail to that country…we shall stop at several cuntreys before we gets there for fresh water I expects you will eare from me in the course of 9 months….You may depend upon My keeping Myselfe from all other Woman for i shall Never Let No other run into my mind for tis onely you My Dear that can Ease me of my Desire. It is not Laving Auld england that grives me it is laving my dear and loving Wife and Children, May God be Mersyful to me."

Mary Ann did not reply to Peter's letters. She herself could not write and probably could not raise the money to pay someone to do it for her. With at least nine months' interval between letters—the time it took for the voyage to Australia and back—a great deal could happen, and it took her 11 years to contact her husband. As late as 1833, Peter still hoped that he and Mary Ann might somehow be together again. He wrote to his brother, telling him how well things had turned out for him. He had

"a good Master and Mistress…. Plenty to eate and drink as good as ever a gentleman in this country…"
and added:

"…so all the Punishment I have in this Country is the thoughts of leaving My frends, My wife and My Dear Dear Children, but I lives in hopes of seeing Old England again."

But with no news from Mary Ann, Peter finally made the decision to marry again,

"a partner which would be a comfort to me in my Bondage."

When Mary Ann finally wrote to her husband seeking a reconciliation, some 11 years after their separation, she was too late. But even

Right An aquatint, c. 1830, of Hobart, Tasmania (known until 1856 as Van Diemen's Land). This is how it would have looked to Withers when he arrived by ship. The British took over the island in 1803 and used it as a penal settlement.

❧ *The Lovers* ❧

PETER WITHERS
(1807–d. ?),
a shoemaker by trade, was born in Wiltshire, southern England. In 1830, at age 23, he was involved in a local "Captain Swing" riot, a protest by farmworkers against poor living conditions, low wages, and the introduction of threshing machines that would put many of them out of work. On January 8, 1831, Withers was sentenced to death, but this was commuted to transportation. Two years later he wrote to his brother from Van Diemen's Land (present-day Tasmania), telling him that he had sent two letters to his wife entreating her to join him. Eleven years passed before Withers received word from her, and by then it was too late; he had taken a new wife and made a new life for himself.

MARY ANN HOBBS
(dates unknown)
married Peter Withers in the parish church of Ramsbury, Wiltshire, on October 28, 1828. She had two children by him, one of them a son named Samuel. Mary Ann had been married for little more than two years when her husband was transported to Tasmania. Unable to write—she signed her marriage certificate with a cross—she did not reply to her husband's letters entreating her and the children to join him in Tasmania. However, in 1844, perhaps with paid help, she sent a letter of reconciliation, only to learn that Withers had remarried. In 1847 a letter from the Colonial Office told her that Peter Withers "was living on the 30 Septr. 1846," but that "no further information can be given respecting him."

though Peter had taken another wife, he wrote kindly and with honesty to Mary Ann:

"I have no property of my own but my wife have property wich she will have in the course of two years and then we have agreed to help you an [sic] the children if God spares our lives. I know that for to eare that I am married is a hard trial for you to bear, but it is no good to tell you a Lye."

Harsh laws had robbed a man of his country and family, and a wife of her husband and financial support. But no hardship could rob them of good hearts.

Fanny Kemble to Pierce Butler

London,
December 1842 or early 1843

Having loved you well enough to give you my life when it was best worth giving—having made you the center of all my hopes of earthly happiness—having never loved any human being as I have loved you, you can never be to me like any other human being, and it is utterly impossible that I should ever regard you with indifference. My whole existence having once had you for its sole object, and all its thoughts, hopes, affections having, in their full harvest, been yours, it is utterly impossible that I should ever forget this—that I should ever forget that you were once my lover and are my husband and the father of my children. I cannot behold you without emotion; my heart still answers to your voice, my blood in my veins to your footsteps.

Left *A photograph of Pierce Butler in middle age.*

Below *The playbill for Fanny's stage debut as Juliet on October 5, 1829. Her father and mother appeared with her in the same production.*

On October 5, 1829, a 20-year-old actress named Fanny Kemble made her stage début at the Theatre Royal, Covent Garden, in London. She was gifted with a beautiful voice and enchanting eyes, and was an instant hit in the part of Juliet in Shakespeare's story of "star-cross'd lovers," *Romeo and Juliet*. Fanny did not know that she too was soon to become a "star-cross'd lover." Three years later, she embarked on an American tour and met the Philadelphia businessman Pierce Butler, the handsome heir to a Georgia cotton fortune. Her poignant letter, recalling the strength of their love, was written in 1842, eight years after they married.

Fanny had no instinctive love of acting. She went on stage out of loyalty to her father, Charles Kemble, the nearly bankrupt actor-manager of the Theatre Royal, in an effort to augment the family fortunes. In 1832 she joined with her father in a potentially profitable American tour.

The United States was still a raw, young country, and Fanny kept a journal of all she saw, the hotels she visited, the things people said and did. She was a mixture of womanly independence and Old World pride, and her comments were often harsh. Received well by American audiences, she gradually adjusted to the new country. It was in Philadelphia, in October 1832, that the general adulation which she inspired everywhere became a more powerful emotion for Pierce Butler, a member of the audience. He was quickly obsessed by Fanny, and she responded warmly to his flattering attentions. Whenever her schedule allowed the time, they went riding together, and Pierce

Above *Fanny Kemble, painted by Thomas Sully in 1833, the year before her marriage to Pierce Butler. She sat for the portrait in Philadelphia, where the couple first met in 1832, when Fanny was touring American theaters.*

followed her tours to Baltimore, New York, and Boston. In Pierce's company Fanny began to consider making the United States her new home. On June 7, 1834, they were married in Philadelphia. The decision was hard for Fanny. Her family's fortunes were closely tied to her popularity on the stage. Like Juliet, forced to choose between family and lover, she chose the lover. She gave up her acting career in favor of staying with Pierce, but she also wept at her wedding. To soften the blow to her father, she gave him the small fortune that she had earned on the tour. Financially, she had made herself totally dependent on Pierce.

Charles Kemble returned to England and the newlyweds settled into life in Philadelphia. Fanny, who was pregnant within a few months, turned her attention to her written impressions of America and began to prepare them for publication. Pierce, reacting to her gibes against his country, suggested she tone down the more hurtful observations. In a clash between tactful silence and uncompromising conscience, Fanny defended her right to say what she really thought. So bitter were their differences surrounding publication of *The Journal of a Residence in America* that Fanny threatened to leave Pierce then and there. Pierce refused to take her threats too seriously, attributing them to postpartum depression after the birth of their daughter Sarah in May 1935. It was not a good start, and worse was to come.

Right *Fanny's receipt for her first salary—she was paid £910 for 182 performances as Juliet in her father's theater in London. In 1830, £910 was a small fortune.*

Theatre Royal, Covent-Garden, 29 May 1830.

Memorandum for £.910 : — : — received by me from the Proprietors of the Theatre Royal, Covent-Garden—amount of my Salary from 5th October 1829 to 28th May 1830.

182 Nights at £.5. — per Night.

Above *Butler Place, Pierce's family home some six miles from Philadelphia, where the newly married Pierce and Fanny lived from January 1835. The house no longer exists.*

Right *A woman with her child hulling rice with a mortar and pestle in a rice field in Georgia near where Fanny lived with Pierce. The sight of enslaved women and children doing manual labor upset Fanny more than anything else she saw there.*

Though a Philadelphian, Pierce was heir to a cotton fortune in Georgia. In 1838, Fanny paid her first visit to the family plantation on Butler's and St. Simon's Islands just off the coast. She was appalled by the conditions of the slaves and by their subservience, and ashamed that she depended on their labor for her well-being. She wrote,

> "*Their nakedness clothes me, and their heavy toil maintains me in a luxurious idleness.*"

Finding herself unable to help them or to influence her husband to change his behavior radically, she began to contemplate leaving Pierce and returning to England. As she wrote,

> "*This is no place for me, since I was not born among slaves and cannot bear to live among them.*"

On their return to Philadelphia, Fanny gave birth to

their second child, Frances Anne (named after Fanny, and known to the family as Fan). In the weeks that followed, the tensions and squabbling between Fanny and Pierce continued. Although they lived in the same house, they reserved most of what they had to say for letters, perhaps the easiest way of communicating things that they found difficult to say face-to-face. Aware that their marriage was in trouble, they both confided in their friend, Elizabeth Sedgwick. It is clear from Pierce's letter to Elizabeth that he believed in the bond of affection between himself and his wife:

"I have never doubted the continuance and strength of her love for me and she should never have doubted mine. I know that our feelings are as strong as when we first loved but cemented and made holy by the birth of our two daughters."

He went on to assure her,

"If we are not happy together, less happy should we be apart."

In 1841, because Fanny's father was very ill, the Butlers and their daughters left the United States for London, where Pierce soon proved himself a spendthrift. Even the suggestion that the part of Fanny's journal covering the South should be published outraged Pierce. Fanny was mortified. Publication would earn much-needed money, for Pierce had yet to inherit his fortune, and his spending was steadily draining their resources. For a year, upheaval followed upheaval. The letter from which the extract is taken dates from this period, when Fanny—torn between love and her need for independence—decided yet again to leave Pierce. However, she stayed, and they returned to Philadelphia, where their lack of money forced them to live in a boarding house.

Finally, in October 1845, Fanny, worn down by years of emotional turmoil, left for England, her marriage in shreds. During their last months together she accused Pierce of adultery, quoting as evidence some letters that she found in his desk; but this accusation was never substantiated and may have been simply an expression of her anger. From the beginning, their love for each other was frustrated by the

Above *Pierce's and Fanny's two daughters, Sarah and Frances (or Fanny), known as "Fan."*

incompatibility of their temperaments. Their efforts to reconcile differences were thwarted by Fanny's determination not to be made an obedient and dependent wife. Neither could make their love work for the other. Fanny wrote to Pierce,

"I have only to regret that I am not other than I am, perhaps I might have been happier than I am, and possessed qualities more acceptable to you than those with which nature and education have endowed me."

In 1848, Pierce began divorce proceedings. The settlement secured the children's financial future but limited Fanny's access to her daughters. Neither Pierce nor Fanny married again. In 1863, Fanny's book, *Journal of a Residence on a Georgian Plantation*, was published in London. On her 80th birthday, Fanny was shown an 1829 engraving of herself as the star-crossed lover, Juliet. She said only,

"I had quite forgotten it."

Zelda Sayre *to* F. Scott Fitzgerald

Spring 1919

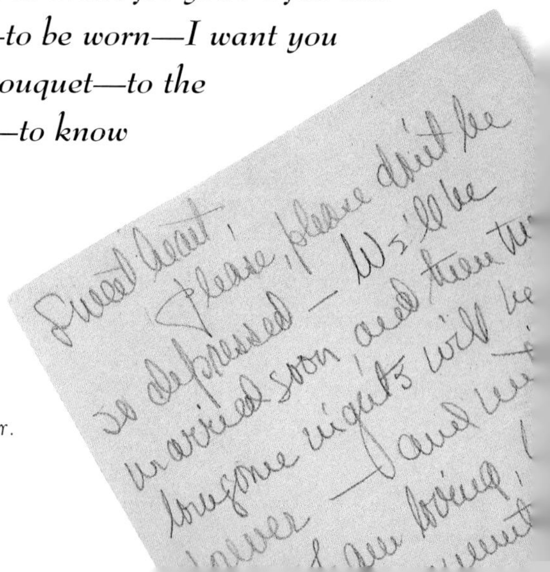

Sweetheart,

Please, please don't be so depressed—
We'll be married soon, and then these lonesome
nights will be over forever—and until we are, I
am loving, loving every tiny minute of the day
and night—Maybe you won't understand this,
but sometimes when I miss you most, it's hardest
to write—and you always know when I make
myself—Just the ache of it all—and I can't tell you.
If we were together, you'd feel how strong it is—you're
so sweet when you're melancholy. I love your sad
tenderness—when I've hurt you—That's one of the reasons I could never
be sorry for our quarrels—and they bothered you so—Those dear, dear
little fusses, when I always tried so hard to make you kiss and forget—

Scott—there's nothing in all the world I want but you—and your
precious love—All the material things are nothing. I'd just hate to live a sordid,
colorless existence—because you'd soon love me less—and less—and I'd do
anything—anything—to keep your heart for my own—I don't want to live—I
want to love first, and live incidentally....Don't—don't ever think of the things
you can't give me—You've trusted me with the dearest heart of all—and it's so
damn much more than anybody else in all the world has ever had—

How can you think deliberately of life without me—If you should die—
O Darling—darling Scott—It'd be like going blind....I'd have no purpose in
life—just a pretty—decoration. Don't you think I was made for you? I feel like
you had me ordered—and I was delivered to you—to be worn—I want you
to wear me, like a watch—charm or a button hole bouquet—to the
world. And then, when we're alone, I want to help—to know
that you can't do anything without me...

All my heart—
I love you

Zelda

One hot Alabama night in July 1918, 23-year-old Francis Scott Fitzgerald, First Lieutenant 67th Infantry and aspiring writer, met the beautiful young Zelda Sayre at a Country Club dance in her hometown, Montgomery. She was a teenage whirlwind, just out of high school, sweeping up the beaus of the town—the "jellybeans" as they were known—in her wake. As he danced with Zelda, the handsome Scott smelled to her:

"like new goods…luxury bound in bales."

Several weeks later Scott seemed to have made up his mind to marry Zelda. A diary entry for September 1918 reads:

"Fell in love on the 7th."

Other diary entries and reports from friends suggest that Scott rushed and dazzled her, calling almost daily and dating her regularly.

When they met, Scott was stationed at Camp Sheridan near Montgomery, awaiting the call to the war in Europe. But the war ended in November, and Scott did not have to go. Instead, still deeply attracted to Zelda as she was to him, he went to New York to pursue the wealth and influence that success as a novelist would bring them both. It was a dream that Zelda shared, a way into a new life. The extracted letter printed here—passionate and edgy—was written just before they got engaged. Scott mailed Zelda his mother's engagement ring in late March 1919.

Back in Montgomery, Zelda was surrounded by suitors whom she encouraged, young men spilling liquor in fast cars. Scott, who was not finding it easy to make a career out of writing advertising copy in New York, was distraught when Zelda broke off their engagement that June. It seemed she wanted their marriage to be founded on self-confidence and success, not failure and poverty. Scott quit his job in advertising and returned to his family home in St. Paul, Minnesota, to rewrite his first novel, *This Side of Paradise*. Scribner's accepted the book for publication in September. Over the next few months Scott visited Zelda several times. For all her reckless behavior, she was in love with him, and they renewed their engagement.

They were married in New York at St. Patrick's Cathedral in April 1920, a month after *This Side of Paradise* had been published to rave reviews and big sales. They became the talk of the town, a golden couple who personified the stylish, reckless living of New York's "Jazz Age" in the Twenties. They were also complex and vulnerable people, who found their role bewildering. Back in 1915 Scott had dropped out of Princeton to write. He was extremely dedicated, working long hours and drinking heavily to relax. Paradoxically, his newfound success threatened the solitude he needed to write. Zelda's role was even

Above *F. Scott Fitzgerald in 1918. He left Princeton University early to take up an army commission, and was eager for action overseas. While he waited, he devoted all his free time to writing the first draft of* This Side of Paradise *on "smeary pencil pages."*

Right *Scott and Zelda at the wheel. Fast cars, liquor, and high living filled their lives during the 1920's.*

Below *Zelda was a constant source of inspiration for Scott. Here the couple are featured on W. E. Hill's dust jacket of* The Beautiful and Damned *(1922), which sold more than 40,000 copies in its first year.*

more tangled. Just after the couple married, a friend of Scott's from Princeton, Alexander McCaig, described her as a,

> *"temperamental, small-town Southern belle,"*

who chewed gum and showed her knees. A year later he had changed his mind. She was,

> *"without doubt the most brilliant and most beautiful young woman I've ever known."*

Scott told him that her ideas figured large in the novel he was currently working on, *The Beautiful and Damned.* Zelda became, in effect, Scott's material. Nearly all his books described variations on their life together, sometimes incorporating bits of her diaries and letters as well. As Zelda said at the time,

> *"Plagiarism begins at home."*

Their daughter, Scottie, was born in October 1921. Meanwhile the wear and tear of life on Long Island,

with its heavy drinking and nonstop high living, began to show in the marriage.

In January 1922, with clinical yet admiring detachment, Scott wrote to the literary critic Edmund Wilson that,

> *"the complete, fine and full-hearted selfishness and chill-mindedness of Zelda"*

enormously influenced his writing. Perhaps the "selfishness" to which Scott referred was Zelda's struggle to realize herself beyond her role in Scott's fiction. She too began to write.

In 1924, in an attempt to restore their disheveled lives and find space for Scott to write, they left New York for France, living first in Paris and then at St. Raphael, a small resort on the Riviera. There, within the beach community of bronzed young men, the Americans befriended a French aviator named Edouard Jozan. To Scott's outrage and shock, Zelda fell in love with Edouard and asked Scott for a divorce. At the beginning of September, just when their crisis seemed to have passed, she overdosed on sleeping pills. The dose was not fatal, and in November, with Zelda recovered and Scott's new novel,

Above *A self-portrait of Zelda made in the early 1940's. She spent a decade struggling against schizophrenia, while Scott was trying to curb his addiction to alcohol. Scott felt her suffering deeply, and used his feelings about it in* Tender Is the Night.

The Great Gatsby, completed—they traveled together to Italy. There Zelda began to paint, a pastime she would maintain for life. Back in Paris in 1928, Zelda took up a new and compulsive interest—ballet. Much to Scott's distress and anger she practiced for hours at a time, straining for:

> *"the flights of the human soul divorced from the person."*

She was 27, far too old to have any real success as a dancer. Not wanting Scott to pay for the ballet lessons, she wrote to earn the money for them. These twin pressures—along with the anxieties they concealed—exhausted her and in 1930 precipitated her first mental breakdown. Zelda moved from clinic to clinic in Europe and the United States with brief periods of fragile stability at home, increasingly apart from, but always in touch with, her husband. Many of their letters from this period are affectionate and nostalgic, Scott reminding her of old friends and Zelda thanking him for gifts of flowers, jewelry, and perfume. A few letters express Scott's fears for her recovery. He saw Zelda's writing as the most destructive of her bids to realize herself. Zelda was his raw

material as well as her own, and who could use it better, the rambling amateur or the fine-honed professional? In the midst of her illness, he insisted,

> *"I want you to stop writing fiction."*

Later, after his death, Zelda dreamed that his voice called to her,

> *"I have lost the woman I put in my book."*

Even when they were fighting a battle of wills, they were fighting more for each other than against each other. As Scott put it,

> *"Liquor on my mouth is sweet to her; I cherish her most extravagant hallucinations."*

Scott died of a heart attack in 1940, while Zelda was still in the hospital. Looking back, she remembered the best things about their time together,

> *"It seems as if he was always planning happiness for Scottie and me."*

In the "golden boom" of Twenties' New York they got too much too soon. Zelda said in 1939,

> *"Nothing could have survived our life."*

❧ *T h e   L o v e r s* ❧

ZELDA SAYRE
(1900–48)
was born in Montgomery, Alabama. Daughter of an Alabama High Court judge, Zelda was strikingly beautiful but wild, intelligent but unevenly educated. She married Scott Fitzgerald in 1920 and they had one daughter, Frances (known as Scottie), in 1921. After several years of high and happy living, financed by Scott's success as a writer and shaped by his drinking, her behavior became more erratic and obsessive, and their relationship more strained. In 1930 she had her first mental breakdown. The years that followed were largely spent in mental institutions, but also saw the publication of her confused and moving novel *Save Me the Waltz* (1932). She had considerable talent, which never quite fulfilled itself. Zelda died in 1948, victim of an asylum fire at the Highland Hospital, Asheville, North Carolina.

FRANCIS SCOTT KEY
FITZGERALD
(1896–1940),
novelist and short story writer, was born in St. Paul, Minnesota. Irish on his mother's side, he was a Catholic and was educated at Princeton University. He gained instant fame with his first novel *This Side of Paradise* (1920). Together with his wife Zelda, he came to represent the "Jazz Age," both in his writing and in his lifestyle, with his wildness, generosity, heavy drinking, partying, and high spending. His finest novel was *The Great Gatsby* (1925), the story of rich financier Jay Gatsby's disastrous love for Daisy Buchanan and a key exploration of "The American Dream." After that the writing came more slowly and the success less surely. He worked periodically as a scriptwriter in Hollywood, where he died of a heart attack in 1940. His final novel, *The Last Tycoon*, was unfinished when he died.

Franz Kafka to Milená Jesenská

c. 1922

No, Milená, I beg you once again to invent another possibility for my writing to you. You mustn't go to the post office in vain, even your little postman— who is he?—mustn't do it, nor should even the postmistress be asked unnecessarily. If you can find no other possibility, then one must put up with it, but at least make a little effort to find one.

Above *Franz Kafka photographed in 1921 when he was 38 years old.*

Last night I dreamed about you. What happened in detail I can hardly remember, all I know is that we kept merging into one another. I was you, you were me. Finally you somehow caught fire. Remembering that one extinguished fire with clothing, I took an old coat and beat you with it. But again the transmutations began and it went so far that you were no longer even there, instead it was I who was on fire and it was also I who beat the fire with the coat. But the beating didn't help and it only confirmed my old fear that such things can't extinguish a fire. In the meantime, however, the fire brigade arrived and somehow you were saved. But you were different from before, spectral, as though drawn with chalk against the dark, and you fell, lifeless or perhaps having fainted from joy at having been saved, into my arms. But here too the uncertainty of transmutability entered, perhaps it was I who fell into someone's arms.

Above *Sketches from Kafka's diary, 1924, in which he wrote: "I am quite certainly writing out of despair about my body and about the future with this body." This theme recurs in his relationship with Milená.*

In 1919 the German-speaking Czech writer Franz Kafka, recuperating from tuberculosis in a sanatorium, received a letter from a 24-year-old journalist from Vienna, Miléna Jesenská. She wanted to translate his enigmatic stories into Czech. Early in 1920 she sent him her first translations, and they began a tormented two-year passion that was conducted almost entirely by correspondence. For Kafka, Miléna's letters were,

> "...the most beautiful thing that ever happened in my life."

Those letters have been lost. Kafka's own undated letters, preserved by Miléna and hidden in Prague during World War II, tell a story with few fixed points. The letter printed here is from near the end of their relationship. The paranoia and uncertainty it expresses—about Miléna's husband finding out, and about the potential sexuality of the relationship—typify Kafka's state of mind throughout the affair.

Initially they wrote in German, Kafka's native language. He later insisted that Miléna write in Czech, since he could only capture her whole personality through her native tongue. After the first Czech letter, Kafka wrote,

> "I see you more clearly, the movements of your body, your hands, so quick, so determined, it's almost a meeting, although when I try to raise my eyes to your face, what breaks into the flow of the letter... is fire and I see nothing but fire."

Kafka found her intensity intriguing, but felt that the fire in her personality burned mainly for her husband, Ernst Polak. In fact, Miléna's relationship with her husband was disintegrating at the time. He excluded her from his social and intellectual life, and made no attempt to hide his affairs with other women. In the face of Ernst's infidelities she reached out to Kafka and confided in him. He responded completely to the sensitive personality that came across in her prose:

> "One leans right back and drinks the letters, oblivious of everything except that one doesn't want to stop drinking."

She was not the first woman in Kafka's life, and he tried to be objective about their future together:

> "I've been engaged twice (three times, if you wish, that's to say twice to the same girl), so I've been separated three times from marriage by only a few days. The first one is completely over...the second is without any prospect of marriage..."

He wanted to marry, he explained, but feared it would affect his writing. For Kafka, marriage was not a way out of loneliness but a vision of security, a vocation in itself:

> "Marrying, founding a family, accepting all the children that come, supporting them in this insecure world and perhaps even guiding them a little, is I am convinced, the utmost a human being can succeed in doing at all."

Such ordinary happiness was beyond Kafka. He was well liked, thoughtful, and generous, but his real life was a surreal fabric of the mind, beset by anxieties. He analyzed every move until no move was possible. In one of his stories he wrote about a man who is fascinated by a spinning top and wants to know how it works. Yet every time he grabs it, it goes dead in his hands. So too, it turned out, with his and Miléna's relationship; it was beautiful in the abstract, but failed to work once it involved physical realities.

Above Miléna, photographed on holiday (date unknown).

After months of writing to each other, Kafka and Milená became impatient to meet face to face. They struggled to arrange a few days or hours together, either in Vienna or Gmünd, on the border between Austria and Czechoslovakia. Kafka was nervous about the meeting, using any excuse to cancel or delay it. In one letter he argued that their ages were the problem. Milená was so young, he protested, and he was nearly 38 (in fact he was 36). In another he objected on the grounds that the nervous strain would be too much for him:

> *"I'm quite definitely not coming, but if I do—it won't happen—shock myself by arriving in Vienna, I'll need neither breakfast nor supper but a stretcher."*

Gradually he came to accept the idea. Feeling excited, but uncertain, he assured Milená,

> *"You don't have to worry; once I get into the coach to Vienna, I'll more than likely get out at Vienna, only the getting in represents difficulties."*

Four days in Vienna in the summer of 1920 was the most physical point in their relationship. Neither had much taste for,

> *"the half-hour in bed—men's business,"*

as Milená called it. Besides Milená was married, and her husband's interest in her seemed reawakened by Kafka's attentions. During the weeks that followed, they discussed over and over again in their letters the problem of whether they could live together or not. In August Milená wrote explicitly that she could not

Above *Milená's translation of Kafka's short story "Der Heizer" (The Stoker), published in 1920 in the Czech literary magazine, Kmen. Kafka wrote to her: "I wouldn't have believed such fidelity was possible in the Czech language."*

leave her husband. Kafka replied that he had known her answer all along:

> *"It was behind nearly all your letters...it was in your eyes."*

Simple domestic love could never be theirs:

> *"We shall never live together, in the same apartment, body to body, at the same table, never, not even in the same town."*

Gradually the letters became less passionate and more like entries in a diary. Kafka's health deteriorated and Milená began to feel that she had added to his anxieties. She suggested a meeting, but he could not bear the pressure of seeing her again, and shortly afterward proposed that they stop writing to each other. He wrote to Milená that he was aware of an

> *"irresistibly strong voice, actually your voice, that's demanding silence from me....These letters are nothing but torture, produced by torture, irremediable...."*

In the end it was Kafka who made the decision that he and Milená should stop seeing each other:

> *"Don't write and avoid meeting me, just fulfill this request for me in silence, it's the only way I can somehow go on living...."*

In fact, he had little more life to live. He died of tuberculosis in 1924, two years after the relationship ended. Milená treasured his letters for the rest of her life.

Below *Kafka sent this postcard of Gmünd to his sister, Ottla, in 1920. He stopped here on his return from meeting Milená in Vienna in June/July. In August Kafka and Milená spent a weekend here together.*

The
❦ *Lovers* ❦

FRANZ KAFKA
(1883–1924)

was one of the most influential novelists of the 20th century. His works powerfully express the anxieties of individuals trapped in a modern society. A Czech-born German, he was brought up in a middle-class Jewish family, the son of a domineering father, Hermann Kafka, and the older brother to three sisters. He studied law at the University of Prague and afterward worked in an insurance company. The frustrated hero-victims of his novels *The Trial* (1925) and *The Castle* (1926) were modeled on his own life, shaped by his profound fear of his father and deep sense of isolation from the world. Delicate, introspective, and prone to depression, he had many unsatisfactory affairs with women. Tuberculosis made Kafka an invalid and forced him to retire in 1922. He died two years later. Other major works include *The Judgment* (1912) and *Metamorphosis* (1915).

MILENÁ JESENSKÁ
(1896–1944)

was the daughter of a Czech nationalist professor who had her interned in a mental clinic for eight months for stealing money from him to give to her lovers. Soon after her release, she married Ernst Polak, a German-speaking Jew, and they settled in Vienna. Neglected by her unfaithful husband, Milená resorted to taking cocaine. To provide herself with independent means, she took up journalism, and in 1919 wrote to Kafka asking permission to translate his works. This triggered an intense correspondence that fulfilled a mutual need for intimacy. They had four days together in Vienna, but Kafka could not sustain the relationship, and Milená did not want to leave her husband. She died in Ravensbruk concentration camp in 1944, a victim of the Holocaust.

Left *The woods above Vienna where Kafka and Milená walked during the happy days that they spent together there.*

Joys & Consolations

"... They are in love,

they have always been in love,

although sometimes

they would have denied it.

And because

they have been in love

they have survived everything

that life could throw

at them ..."

ERNEST HAVEMANN,
"Love and Marriage," LIFE
September 29, 1961

Pliny the Younger to his wife, Calpurnia

c. A.D. 100

You say that you are feeling my absence very much, and your only comfort when I am not there is to hold my writings in your hand and often put them in my place by your side. I like to think that you miss me and find relief in this sort of consolation. I, too, am always reading your letters, and returning to them again and again as if they were new to me—but this only fans the fire of my longing for you. If your letters are so dear to me, you can imagine how I delight in your company; do write as often as you can, although you give me pleasure mingled with pain.

Above *Rings depicting clasping hands were a common gift of devotion exchanged by a couple once they were engaged to be married.*

Left *A typical Roman marriage ceremony. The groom is holding the marriage contract, which would have been drawn up before the ceremony.*

In the nine books of personal letters that Pliny the Younger published during his lifetime, he made his bid for immortality. The letters reveal both the public man he wanted remembered—a successful lawyer, a keen observer of human nature, and an efficient administrator—and in letters such as the one printed here, the private man: the devoted husband of a young and loving wife.

Pliny the Younger was born in Comum (present-day Como), beside the beautiful lakes of northern Italy, in A.D. 61 or 62 and educated in Rome. In A.D. 79 his uncle, the writer Pliny the Elder, was killed in the eruption of Vesuvius that destroyed the city of Pompeii. He left a will formally adopting his nephew as his heir. The following year Pliny began to practice law. He gained a reputation for skill and honesty in handling civil cases concerning disputed inheritances; success in civic and state administration followed, and he became a consul, the highest office of state, at the exceptionally early age of 39.

By that time he had already been married twice. To his great grief, both his wives died childless, the second in A.D. 97. Having lived through the cruel reign of the emperor Domitian, he was acutely aware of the uncertainty of life and longed for a child to continue his name. The emperor Trajan, who had a good working relationship with Pliny, granted him in A.D. 98 the privileges of extra land reserved for parents of three children. He wrote in reply:

"Still more now do I long for children of my own, though I wanted them even during those dark evil days now past, as you may know from my having married twice.... Now is the time I would wish to be a father when my happiness need know no fear!

Then he married Calpurnia. He was 39; she was probably not much more than 14, not unusual for new wives in a society where childbearing was of key importance to marriage. Calpurnia was an orphan, the granddaughter of Calpurnius Fabatus, a prosperous citizen in Comum, who looked after Pliny's estates there. Pliny loved "our darling Comum" and wrote affectionately of the honesty and simplicity of its people. It is understandable that he chose to take as his bride a girl from a family he knew and trusted rather than a girl from Rome.

Calpurnia was everything Pliny had hoped for in a young wife. He praised her intelligence, her devotion, and her skill at looking after their home. In a

Right *We know from one of Pliny's letters (extracted overleaf) that Calpurnia—like the young woman playing her kithara in this mid–first century B.C. fresco from the villa Boscoreale, near Pompeii—played a lyre, and set some of his verses to music.*

letter to his wife's aunt, Calpurnia Hispulla, who had brought her up, he added:

"In addition, this love has given her an interest in literature: she keeps copies of my works to read again and again and even learn by heart. She is so anxious when she knows that I am going to plead in court, and so happy when all is over! (She arranges to be kept informed of the sort of reception and applause I receive and what verdict I win in the case.)…She has even set my verses to music and sings them, to the accompaniment of her lyre, with no musician to teach her but the best of masters, love."

It pleased him, he wrote in closing the letter, that Calpurnia did not love him for his looks, which in the course of time would decay, but for his "aspirations to fame." He was also moved by the fact that she seemed to understand his longing to be remembered, to gain immortality through his professional reputation and writings.

He also hoped for children, who would continue the family line and could pass on their memories of their parents to others. When Calpurnia miscarried, Pliny wrote sadly to her grandfather:

"Being young and inexperienced, she did not realize she was pregnant…and did several things which were better left undone. She has had a severe lesson, and paid for her mistake by seriously endangering her life…. Your desire for great-grandchildren cannot be keener than mine for children. Their descent from both of us should make their road to office easier; I can leave them a well-known name and an established ancestry, if only they may be born and turn our present grief to joy."

To Calpurnia's aunt he wrote:

"we build our hopes on her, and she has been spared."

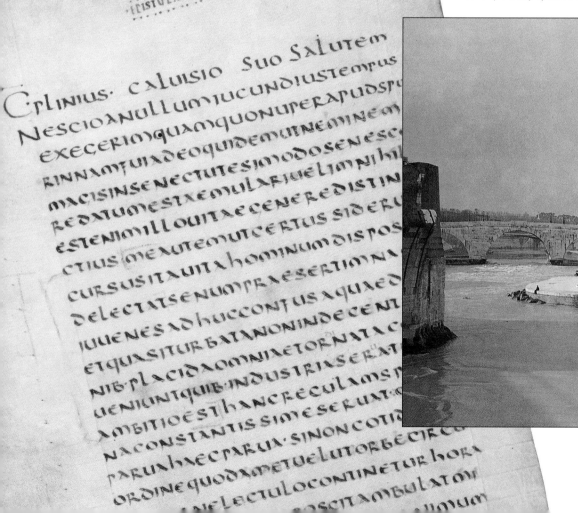

Left *The earliest-known transcription of one of Pliny's letters appears in a fifth-century codex. Altogether Pliny published nine books of selected private letters (c. 100–109). A tenth book contained formal addresses to the emperor Trajan, and Trajan's replies.*

Below *The banks of the River Tiber in Rome. One of Pliny's responsibilities was to ensure the Tiber's banks were kept clean. He also administered the drainage board of the city of Rome.*

Their hopes for children were not fulfilled. Yet the relationship between Pliny and Calpurnia deepened. The letters he wrote to her when they were separated were not formal communications; they used the language of lovers. In the one printed here, Pliny responded to Calpurnia's pain at separation, not only because he knew how intensely she felt it, but because he felt it too. In another letter he wrote,

> *"You cannot believe how much I miss you. I love you so much, and we are not used to separation. So I stay awake most of the night thinking of you, and by day I find my feet carrying me...to your room...then finding it empty I depart, as sick and sorrowful as a lover locked out."*

When Pliny published his letters to Calpurnia, he told the world that their marriage was no formal exchange of contracts based on property, but something central to his life. To feel a lover's romantic passion was for him, a Roman dignitary, a cause for pride, not shame; Calpurnia was rightfully a partner in his bid for immortality.

Left The forum in Rome, where Pliny delivered his speeches in both the civil law courts and the political court that tried provincial officials for extortion. In A.D. 93 he became praetor, and in 100 gained the top administrative position of consul.

❧ *The Lovers* ❧

GAIUS PLINIUS CAECILIUS SECUNDUS

(A.D. 61/62 – c. 113), Roman lawyer and writer known as Pliny the Younger, left a collection of letters that gives the most complete picture available of public and private life in Rome at the end of the 1st century. He was born in northern Italy at Novum Comum (now Como) and adopted as heir by his uncle, the scientist and historian Pliny the Elder. Practicing law from the age of 18, his honesty and financial skills brought him success in inheritance cases and as the prosecutor of corrupt officials. His various administrative posts included president of the board in charge of Rome's drainage, head of the military and senatorial treasuries, and the high state offices of praetor in 93 and consul in 100. In 111 he was sent by the emperor Trajan to investigate municipal incompetence and corruption in the Black Sea provinces of Bithynia and Pontus, but died there two years later at the age of 50. Pliny married three times, his first two wives dying young and childless. His marriage to Calpurnia took place in A.D. 100, the year he became consul. His wide interests included literature, civil engineering, practical farm management, building plans for his villas (including elaborate watering systems for the gardens), and the quiet beauties of landscape and nature.

CALPURNIA

(c. A.D. 86 – d. ?), like Pliny, was born in Comum. Orphaned at an early age, she was brought up by her wealthy grandfather, Calpurnius Fabatus, the manager of Pliny's large estates, and by her aunt Calpurnia Hispulla. She married Pliny when she was probably in her early teens, and traveled with him to Bithynia. In his last surviving letter, he told the emperor Trajan that he had issued her a permit (which he should not have done without the emperor's permission) enabling her to return home quickly so that she could be with her bereaved aunt after the death of her grandfather. While she was away, Pliny himself died.

Mozart to his wife, Constanze

Mainz
October 17, 1790

*PS.—While I was writing the last page, tear after tear fell on the paper.
But I must cheer up—catch!—An astonishing number of kisses are
flying about—The deuce!—I see a whole crowd of them! Ha! Ha!...
I have just caught three—They are delicious!—You can still answer this
letter, but you must address your reply to Linz, Poste Restante—That is
the safest course. As I do not yet know for certain whether I shall go to
Regensburg, I can't tell you anything definite. Just write on the cover that
the letter is to be kept until called for. Adieu—Dearest, most beloved little
wife—Take care of your health—and don't think of walking into town. Do
write and tell me how you like our new quarters—Adieu. I kiss you
millions of times.*

Above *Constanze Mozart, painted by her brother-in-law, Joseph Lange, shortly after her marriage.*

Left *A letter from Mozart to Constanze dated June 6, 1791, the year he died. The original letter belonging to the scribbled postscript printed above no longer exists.*

W olfgang Amadeus Mozart, one of the finest composers the world has ever known, had two great loves in his life: the first was music; and the second was Constanze Weber, whom he married in Vienna on August 4, 1782. She was 20, he was 26.

By the time they married, Mozart's life had already been a long succession of journeys in search of a patron who would free him from financial insecurity and allow him to devote all his energy to composing music. His concert tours began in Salzburg, where he was acclaimed as a musical prodigy at the age of five. He and his elder sister, Maria-Anna, performed in the courts and cathedrals of many of Europe's greatest cities: Munich, Augsburg, Mainz, Frankfurt, Paris, London, and Vienna. In 1772, Mozart at 16 had already written 25 symphonies and his first string quartets. His travels brought him much honor, but not much money, and he tended to be extravagant with what little he earned.

It was in September 1777, while staying in Manneheim with his mother, that Mozart first met Constanze's family, the Webers. He fell in love with her elder sister, Aloysia, a singer of some promise but little experience. Mozart made grand plans to take her to Italy and start her in a career in opera, but his father Leopold, who never trusted the Weber family,

Above A detail from an unfinished portrait of Mozart painted by Joseph Lange in 1789–90. Constanze thought that it was the best likeness of the composer painted during his lifetime.

persuaded him against it. A year later Aloysia's feelings for Mozart had cooled, and he wrote to his father on December 29, 1778,

"I can only weep. I have far too sensitive a heart." Nevertheless, Mozart stayed in close touch with the family, and on December 15, 1781, he wrote again to his father revealing his plans to marry:

"Owing to my disposition, which is more inclined to a peaceful and domesticated existence than to revelry, I, who from my youth up have never been accustomed to look after my belongings, linen clothes and so forth, cannot think of anything more necessary to me than a wife….A bachelor in my opinion is only half alive."

Below Mozart and Constanze's marriage certificate, signed by the couple and dated August 4, 1782. Leopold Mozart strongly objected to his son's choice of bride, and the whole family joined in his protest by staying away from the ceremony.

His attention had now turned to Aloysia's sister, dark-eyed Constanze, with her pretty figure and,

> *"the kindest heart in the world....I love her and she loves me with all her heart."*

Mozart brought to his marriage an engaging personality, limitless talent, and plenty of optimism, but few prospects. He promised her family that if he did not marry Constanze within three years he would pay her 300 gulden every year for the rest of his life.

At their wedding in St. Stephen's Cathedral in Vienna, Mozart and Constanze wept, as did the congregation, and the priest. It was a marriage of deep affection and understanding, both much needed through their years together. Constanze was frequently ill and often with child. In nine years she gave birth to six children, only two of whom survived. Though Mozart probably was, as his great friend, the composer Joseph Haydn, described him,

> *"the greatest composer now living in the world,"*

Above *A view of Vienna with the spire of St. Stephen's Cathedral in the distance. Mozart and Constanze were married there, and Mozart's funeral service also took place in the cathedral in 1791 before he was taken out to the suburban cemetery of St. Marx, to be buried in an unmarked grave.*

he was struggling financially. His career was at the mercy of musical fashion in Vienna, and he was often forced to go on tour in order to pay the doctor's bills for Constanze. Constanze's fondness for her husband and unfailing belief in him were put to the test. Two days before the opening night of Mozart's new opera, *Don Giovanni*, in Prague in 1787, Mozart had not yet written the overture. The more worried the opera's company and producers became, the more carefree Mozart seemed to be. On the last evening, at about midnight, he began to write. Constanze helped to keep him awake by telling him stories, and sustained his energy by making him drink quantities of punch. When he got too tired to work she said he should sleep on the sofa for an hour and she would wake him. But he slept so soundly that she let him sleep until five in the morning. The copyist was due at seven o'clock, and Mozart finished the overture just in time.

Printed here is the postscript to a letter that Mozart wrote to Constanze at the spa town of Baden, where she was seeking a health cure in 1790. He was writing from Mainz while on tour. The words of the letter, full of joy and affection,

Above A draft of the piano concerto K467a, written in Mozart's hand in the 1770's. The manuscript is covered with calculations, showing the extent of his financial worries.

Left The only two of Mozart's six children to survive, painted by Hans Hansen c. 1798. Karl Thomas (right) was born in 1784, Franz Xaver Wolfgang in 1791.

seem to dance with life like the notes of his music. In fact, few people lived or composed with a greater emotional energy than Mozart. Yet he longed for peace and quiet. Marriage—difficult as it was, with lack of money, Constanze's sickness, and his own health problems—consoled him. Two weeks earlier on the same tour Mozart had written affectionately to Constanze from Frankfurt,

> *"I fear…I am in for a restless life….Well it is probable that my concert will not be a failure. I wish it were over, if only to be nearer the time when I shall once more embrace my love."*

Whenever they were apart, Mozart and Constanze exchanged loving letters. He kept a portrait of her in front of him as he wrote, and delighted in the letters she would send to every town where he stayed. But the pressures on him grew. Desperate for money, he undertook engagements in Frankfurt in September 1790, but it was much against his will. Writing to Constanze, he explained:

> *"Perhaps if you were with me I might possibly take more pleasure in the kindness of those I meet here. But, as it is, everything seems so empty."*

Mozart's health worsened. In 1791 he was working on his opera *The Magic Flute* when "a mysterious stranger"—now widely believed to be Count F. von Walsegg-Stuppach—left an anonymous letter commissioning him to write the score for a requiem mass. As he worked on the composition he became obsessed with the idea that he was writing a mass for his own funeral. Constanze tried to calm him and to stop him from working so hard. She even took the unfinished score away from him. As his condition deteriorated, his greatest worry was about Constanze's

future. Just before he died, an hour after midnight on December 5, 1791, he said to his sister-in-law, Sophie Weber,

> *"I already have the taste of death on my tongue, and who can support my dearest Constanze if you do not stay?"*

❧ *The Lovers* ❧

WOLFGANG AMADEUS MOZART
(1756–91)
was born in Salzburg, the son of Leopold Mozart and Anna Maria Pertl. From the age of five he performed all over Europe with his sister, Maria-Anna. In 1763 alone they toured Bavaria, Austria, and Hungary. By 1772 he had composed 25 symphonies and two string quartets. He was appointed honorary concert master to the court in Salzburg in 1774, and after more tours—to Italy, Manneheim, and Paris—and a spell as court organist in Salzburg (1778–80), he moved to Vienna in 1781. Mozart wrote most of his best work in the years that followed: 12 piano concertos (1784–86); six quartets; and the operas *The Marriage of Figaro* (1786), *Don Giovanni* (1787), and *Cosi Fan Tutte* (1790). In 1791, the year of the *Requiem* and *The Magic Flute*, he died of heart failure, at age 35.

CONSTANZE WEBER
(1762–1842)
was the third of four daughters of Fridolin Weber, a musical copyist. Constanze's elder sister, Aloysia, a soprano, was romantically involved with Mozart for a short time when the family lived in Manneheim. After the death of her father, Constanze moved with her mother and younger sister, Sophie, to Vienna, where her courtship with Mozart began. She married him on August 4, 1782, in St. Stephen's Cathedral, and bore him six children, only two of whom—Franz Xaver Wolfgang and Karl Thomas—survived. Constanze was too ill to attend Mozart's funeral. After his death she was granted a pension by the emperor, Leopold II, and she soon married again, this time to a Danish diplomat, Georg Nikolaus von Nissen who became Mozart's biographer. She died in Salzburg in 1842.

Matthew Flinders to his wife, Ann

January 7, 1802

My dearest friend, thou adducest my leaving thee to follow the call of my profession, as a poor proof of my affection for thee. Dost thou not know, my beloved, that we could have barely existed in England? That both thou and me must have been debarred of even necessaries: unless we had given up our independence to have procured them from perhaps unwilling friends. It was only upon the certainty of obtaining an employment, the produce of which would be adequate to thy support as well as my own, that I dared to follow the wishes of my heart and press thee to be mine. Heaven knows with what sincerity and warmth of affection I have loved thee—how anxiously I look forward to the time when I may return to thee, and how earnestly I labour that the delight of our meeting may be no more clouded with the fear of a long parting. Do not then, my beloved, adduce the following of the dictates of necessity as my crime.... Let not unavailing sorrow increase thy malady, but look my dear Ann to the happy side. See me engaged, successfully thus far, in the cause of science and followed by the good wishes and approbation of the world.

Matt.ᵂ Flinders

Above A miniature on ivory of Matthew Flinders by Helena G. De Courcy (date unknown).

Above left A letter that Flinders wrote to his wife six months after the extract shown above (the original of which no longer exists). Letters such as these kept their love strong throughout their long years of separation.

On January 25, 1801, 26-year-old Matthew Flinders was given command of H.M.S. *Investigator*, and charged with exploring and making a detailed survey of all the unknown parts of the Australian coastline. Before he left, he had one very important matter to settle. He had long been in love with his childhood friend, Ann Chappelle. With this new commission, he could at last afford to marry her, and on April 17, 1801—unbeknownst to the Admiralty—they tied the knot. Flinders planned to take Ann with him and settle her in Port Jackson, New South Wales, the future base for his exploration. But when his patron, Sir Joseph Banks, learned that Ann was aboard ship, he and the Admiralty made Flinders choose between his command and Ann's company. Late in May, Flinders wrote to Banks:

"I am afraid to risk their Lordships' ill opinion, and Mrs. F. will return to her friends immediately our sailing orders arrive."

Ann did not see her husband for almost 10 years. The letter extracted here is one of many in which they pondered their decision and consoled each other.

Matthew and Ann had an understanding for at least six years before their marriage, and were accustomed to long periods of separation. In one of her letters to him during his first exploration of Australian waters (1795–1801), Ann told him that she was studying geography. It was, she wrote,

"…most necessary to keep in touch with thee, but indeed thou art beyond geography. Thy descriptions of the new land are enthralling, I read them over and over again with gladness. Thou hast asked me if I would ever be willing that we should make our home there. Believe me, dear Matthew, I should be more than willing, for if thou canst find happiness and beauty in that wild strand, so shall I. But as thou sayest, this is but a dream. We know not what the future will bring."

Left *Ann Flinders devoted much time to painting watercolors of plants, including species collected during Flinders's voyages.*

Below *Between 1802 and 1803, during his circumnavigation of Australia, Flinders charted some 2,700 miles of unknown coastline with such accuracy that very few alterations were needed in later years. This chart, based on his surveys, was published in 1829.*

On July 17, 1801, H.M.S. *Investigator* sailed under Flinders's command. He wrote to his wife in Lincolnshire, imploring her to

> "...*write to me constantly, write me pages and volumes. Tell me what thou wearest, tell me thy dreams, anything, so do but talk to me and of thyself.*"

After many adventures, the slow work of mapping the 12,000 miles of coast was completed. The *Investigator*, which was old when Flinders set out, gradually rotted under him, and in 1803 he decided to return to England aboard H.M.S. *Porpoise* to bring back a new ship. More than anything, he wanted to see Ann again. He wrote to a friend, Mrs. Macarthur, in Paramatta in July 1803:

> "*Adieu my dear Madam—I am going home with the promise of being attended by fortune's smiles, and with the delightful prospect of enfolding one to whom my return will be a return of happiness. Be propitious, kind fortune, as heretofore and fail me not at this delightful anxious period.*"

About 750 miles north-northeast of Sydney, Flinders's new ship was wrecked, and he was forced to continue

Above H.M.S. Investigator, *moored off the south coast of western Australia (formerly New Holland), painted by William Westall. Flinders reached these uncharted waters in January 1802, the month he wrote the letter extracted here to Ann.*

his voyage to England on the small schooner *Cumberland*. She was a difficult boat to handle and was in poor condition. On September 24, 1803, he wrote to Governor King that she was

> "...*exceedingly crank...very leaky. I am now sitting on the locker with my knees up to my chin for a table to write on, and in momentary expectation of the sea coming down the companion.*"

To Ann he wrote:

> "*Writing here is like writing on horseback on a rainy day.*"

Having nursed the *Cumberland* well across the Indian Ocean, Flinders was forced to put into Ile de France (present-day Mauritius). This was French territory, and Britain and France were at war. Because he arrived in such a tiny boat, Flinders's documents and safe-conducts as an explorer were viewed with suspicion by General Decaen, who was in charge of the island. Flinders was held first as a spy, and then as a guest, while his case was referred to Paris. As time passed, he learned too much about the strategically important island to be released in time of war, with the result that his detention lasted for six years. He made good friends among the French on the island, but he was sustained most of all by Ann's letters:

"I sigh for them as the most desired of blessings,"
he wrote. He imagined her response to his own letters:

"Happy letter! Happy seal! They will be received by thee with joy, perhaps receive a kiss. O that I were freed from the bond of my parole and could as easily be transported to thee. Still, my beloved, entertain hope. Misfortunes must sometimes have end, and what happiness will be ours when they cease."

Flinders was eventually released on June 13, 1810, but his health was broken by his long captivity. He sailed immediately for England, arriving on October 23.

For whatever reasons—whether because he had been too friendly to the French, or because some of his decisions on the voyages were questioned—the officials in the Admiralty did not give Flinders the financial reward he expected. He spent the next few years writing the story of his momentous explorations, which was published as *A Voyage to Terra Australis*. In 1812 Ann gave birth to their daughter, Anne. Two years later Matthew lay unconscious on his deathbed. His wife placed the first printed copy of his book in his hand so that he might at least

❧ The Lovers ❧

MATTHEW FLINDERS
(1774–1814)
was born in Lincolnshire in northeast England, to a surgeon of Flemish origin. At 15 he joined the navy and in 1791 sailed as a midshipman aboard H.M.S. *Providence* under the notorious Captain Bligh. In 1794 he rejoined his first ship, H.M.S. *Bellerophon*, which was victorious in battle against the French at Brest. In 1795 he sailed to Australia, where he and fellow navigator George Bass explored and mapped the area of Port Jackson, New South Wales. Flinders married in 1801 and set sail again to Australia as captain of H.M.S *Investigator*. Returning in 1803, he was detained on Mauritius by the French until 1810. He spent his final years, dogged by ill health, writing *A Voyage to Terra Australis* and died in 1814.

ANN CHAPPELLE
(1770–1852)
was the stepdaughter of the Reverend. W. Tyler, rector of Brothertoft in Lincolnshire, England. Her own father had died at sea. She must have formed an attachment to Matthew Flinders before he sailed to Australia in 1795, as he named a group of islands off the coast of Tasmania the Chappell[e] Isles. They married on April 17, 1801. Three months later, the Admiralty refused her permission to sail with Flinders to Australia. She did not see her husband again for almost 10 years. From October 1810 until Flinders's death in 1814, they lived in London. A daughter, Anne, was born in 1812, the future mother of Sir William Matthew Flinders Petrie, the famous archeologist and Egyptologist.

feel his life's work. He died the next day. A joy and consolation to him throughout their long separation and short time together, Ann later wrote:

"Respecting my union with my beloved…I think that I may say that during the period we were permitted to live together, not a cloud cast a shadow over the sunshine of our affections, and each day seemed to rivet the attachment more firmly."

CAPTAIN MATTHEW FLINDERS, R.N,
OF DONINGTON, 1774 - 1814
FIRST CIRCUMNAVIGATOR OF AUSTRALIA
WAS MARRIED IN THIS CHURCH TO
ANN CHAPPELLE
(STEPDAUGHTER OF REV. WM. TYLER
WHO LIVED IN THIS PARISH)
17 APRIL 1801
THIS STONE WAS CUT FROM THE AREA OF PORT
PHILIP BAY AND PRESENTED BY THE STATE
OF VICTORIA, AUSTRALIA, 1974.
LINCOLNSHIRE & SOUTH HUMBERSIDE ARTS

Left *A plaque commemorating the marriage of Matthew Flinders and Ann Chappelle stands outside Partney Church, Lincolnshire. Three months of married life together was followed by 10 years of separation.*

Right *Flinders's birthplace in Donington, Lincolnshire. He named many places in Australia after towns back home, including Cape Donington. He was also the first person to name the continent "Australia."*

John Constable to Maria Bicknell

East Bergholt. February 27, 1816

I received your letter my ever dearest Maria, this morning. You know my anxious disposition too well not to be aware how much I feel at this time. At the distance we are from each other every fear will obtrude itself on my mind. Let me hope that you are not really worse than your kindness, your affection, for me make you say…I think… that no more molestation will arise to the recovery of your health, which I pray for beyond every other blessing under heaven.

Above *John Constable, a self-portrait in pencil, dated 1806.*

Let us…think only of the blessings that providence may yet have in store for us and that we may yet possess. I am happy in love—an affection exceeding a thousand times my deserts, which has continued so many years, and is yet undiminished.…Never will I marry in this world if I marry not you. Truly can I say that for the seven years since I avowed my love for you, I have…foregone all company, and the society of all females (except my own relations) for your sake.

I am still ready to make my sacrifice for you…I will submit to any thing you may command me—but cease to respect, to love and adore you I never can or will. I must still think that we should have married long ago—we should have had many troubles—but we have yet had no joys, and we could not have starved.…Your FRIENDS *have never been without a hope of parting us and see what that has cost us both—but no more. Believe me, my beloved & ever dearest Maria, most faithfully yours*

Left *John's letter, and Maria's wedding ring from October 1816.*

The certainty of love in a relationship can carry it through the strongest opposition and heaviest financial hardship. This was certainly true for the 19th-century English painter, John Constable, and the woman he eventually married, Maria Bicknell. Seven years of courtship elapsed before circumstances allowed them to marry in October 1816. The letter extracted here was written a few months before their wedding. Through all their troubles—her failing health and his poverty—they were sustained by their steadfast devotion to each other.

John and Maria met, probably in 1800, in the village of East Bergholt, in Suffolk. At the time, 12-year-old Maria lived in London, where her father was solicitor to the Admiralty, a post that provided the family with a reasonable income. She came to East Bergholt to visit the village rector, Dr. Rhudde, who was her maternal grandfather. The Constable family were already well-established in the village. John's father owned a prosperous local mill and acres of surrounding farmland. Because he earned his living in "trade," not in a "profession" such as law or the church, the Constables belonged to a different class from that of the Bicknells. When he met Maria, John was 24 years old, twice her age. Although he was trained to follow in his father's footsteps, he had chosen instead to be a painter. He already showed considerable promise, and had hopes of one day becoming famous. Until such time, however, he was scarcely able to earn a decent living. Furthermore, he thoroughly disliked painting portraits, the easiest way for a painter of the time to earn money. John painted landscapes in a new and original way, working directly from nature to recreate the real English countryside rather than the highly idealized Italianate skies that were so popular at the time.

Throughout Maria's teenage years the couple became increasingly fond of each other. As good-natured, sensible people in love, nothing should have kept John

Above Maria Bicknell, painted in oils by her future husband in the same year that the couple married. This was one of the few portraits that Constable took pleasure in finishing. On the whole he shunned portrait painting in favor of English landscapes.

Above In an effort to please Maria's grandfather, Dr. Rhudde, Constable presented him with a watercolor of his church in East Bergholt, with this label on the reverse side.

and Maria apart. But Maria's father worried about entrusting his daughter to an artist with little money and doubtful prospects, and her grandfather objected to the family being joined to people in trade. John and Maria, sure that things would eventually work out, settled down to wait, writing affectionate letters of support to each other. On the few occasions when they met, John dutifully paid his respects to the obstructive rector and the hesitant, discouraging Mr. Bicknell. In November 1811, Maria wrote to John that her father's,

"…only objection would be on that necessary article Cash, what can we do?"

John realized that if he was ever going to earn enough money for them to marry, he must paint portraits. But this was not always

131

easy. When a certain Lady Heathcote commissioned him to copy a portrait of her, John wrote to Maria:

"she will not sit to me though she wants many alterations from the original—but I can have prints, drawings and miniatures, locks of hair to do without end."

Probably the only really successful portrait John painted was an exquisite one of Maria done in 1816 before they were married. In a letter to her, which is mostly about the portrait, he wrote,

"I never had an idea before of the real pleasure that a portrait could offer."

After seven years of cautious waiting and letter writing, their situation became intolerable. When John, trying to be helpful, intervened in a Bicknell family matter, Dr. Rhudde was outraged. The incident was trivial, but John and Maria realized that her family would use any excuse to keep them apart. The letter extracted here brings together all their worries about Maria's health, their lack of money, and family opposition, and clearly expresses their steadfast and mutual love in the face of adversity.

In May 1816, John's father died. In his will he left his son enough money for him seriously to consider marriage; not a fortune, but just enough to support a frugal lifestyle. Disregarding the protests of the Bicknells, they planned the future together. Maria asked John what she should wear for the wedding. Still in mourning, he advised black, adding:

"I should think it advisable not to spend your money in clothes, for we have it not to waste in plumb cake, or any nonsense whatsoever."

He also mapped out for her an idea of what their life together would be like, writing,

"You are not coming to wealth, but life comes once and is soon over…riches will not of themselves bring happiness….We love one another and can we have a greater blessing?"

The couple married on October 2, 1816, in London. Maria's father objected to the last and the Reverend Dr. Rhudde remained stonily silent. Neither of them came to the ceremony.

Constable's reputation as a painter grew slowly during the 1820's, but he was never fashionable in his own lifetime. A small legacy to Maria on Dr. Rhudde's death brought them a little more money, and in time they had seven children. In a letter to a friend written in 1824 John enthused,

"My wife is quite well—never saw her better and more active and cheerful. My children are lovely and much grown. John I am sorry to say is a genius and all my children are good tempered."

In March 1828, Maria's father died, leaving in his will the enormous sum of £40,000 to be divided between Maria and her sister. At last John and Maria were financially secure; John was freed from painting portraits, and they no longer needed to skimp and save. Sadly, they had little time to enjoy their prosperity. During the fall of 1828 Maria finally succumbed to tuberculosis and died on November 23. John, who mourned for Maria for the rest of his life, described his wife as a:

"departed Angel…a devoted, sensible, industrious religious mother who was all affection."

They had lived well together without wealth or station, but with courage and devotion.

JOHN CONSTABLE
(1776–1837)

came to dominate English landscape painting in the late 19th century. At the time of his death he was relatively unknown, but admiration for the freshness of his English landscapes soared during the Victorian period. He was born in East Bergholt, Suffolk, a village that he made famous through his scenes of local rural life, and he remained passionately fond of the Suffolk countryside throughout his career. As a young man Constable learned about the practicalities of farming from his father, but showed an enthusiasm for painting, and a marked reluctance to follow in his father's trade. He worked constantly at improving his sketching, and in his mid-20's began to develop his own realistic style. He showed the same sense of purpose in his courtship of Maria Bicknell, whom he married against the wishes of her family. In the years following their marriage he produced his best work, often of Suffolk scenes, including *Stratford Mill* (1820), *The Hay-wain* (1821), and *View on the Stour near Dedham* (1822). As Maria's health failed he painted more somber views with stormy skies—*Hadleigh Castle* (1829) and *Salisbury Cathedral from the Meadows* (1831).

MARIA BICKNELL
(1788–1828)

was the delicate, sickly daughter of a middle-class professional London family. She fell in love with John Constable in 1809, but her family opposed a union with an impecunious artist, and their objections delayed the marriage until 1816. The couple established a home in London, but beginning in 1819 Maria's health failed steadily, and they took houses in Hampstead and Brighton in an effort to move Maria out of the city to places where the air was cleaner. The seven children that she bore during her 12-year marriage must also have taken a heavy toll on her health. Maria died of tuberculosis in November 1828.

Above *Wivenhoe Park, 1816, was one of three landscapes commissioned by a local family, just at the time when John and Maria wanted desperately to raise enough money to marry. With* The Quarters *and* Alresford Hall, *the three rural views paid for their honeymoon.*

Below *Two of Constable's children (probably John Charles, born 1817, and Maria Louisa, born 1819) playing at being a coach-driver and passenger, from a pen and ink watercolor by their father. The sketch is inscribed "all this is entirely his own invention—a little mite inside."*

Sophia Peabody to Nathaniel Hawthorne

December 31, 1839

Best Beloved,—I send you some allumettes wherewith to kindle the taper. There are very few but my second finger could no longer perform extra duty. These will serve till the wounded one be healed, however. How beautiful is it to provide even this slightest convenience for you, dearest! I cannot tell you how much I love you, in this back-handed style. My love is not in this attitude,—it rather bends forward to meet you.

What a year has this been to us! My definition of Beauty is, that it is love, and therefore includes both truth and good. But those only who love as we do can feel the significance and force of this.

My ideas will not flow in these crooked strokes. God be with you. I am very well, and have walked far in Danvers this cold morning. I am full of the glory of the day. God bless you this night of the old year. It has proved the year of our nativity. Has not the old earth passed away from us?—are not all things new?

Your Sophie

Above *Sophia Peabody in an engraving by S. A. Schoff, from a portrait probably painted by Chester Harding (date unknown).*

Left *A page from Sophia's Cuban journal, written in May 1834 during her 18-month stay to improve her health. The sketch is of a Night-blooming Cereus.*

T he letter printed here was written during the long courtship of Nathaniel Hawthorne and Sophia Peabody.

Nathaniel first met Sophia at her home in Salem, Massachusetts, in November 1837. He was a writer of 33. She was 28, a semi-invalid with a talent for painting. The two families were neighbors in Salem, where an ancestor of Nathaniel's, John Hathorne (Nathaniel added the "w" in Hawthorne) had been a judge in the witchcraft trials of 1692. Sophia's sister, Elizabeth, first invited the reclusive Nathaniel and his sisters to visit. In the biography by Edwin Haviland Miller, *Salem Is My Dwelling Place*, she is reported to have said to her sister:

"O Sophia, you must get up and dress and come down. The Hawthornes are here and you never saw anything so splendid—he is handsomer than Lord Byron."

Even with such an introduction, or perhaps because of it, Sophia stayed upstairs in her bedroom while handsome Nathaniel with

"something of the hawk eye about him,"

visited downstairs. When, on a later visit, Sophia did venture downstairs, Nathaniel invited her to call on his sisters one evening. Sophia, who was a victim of almost daily headaches that kept her indoors, said she never went out in the evenings.

"I wish you would, "

Hawthorne replied.

From this beginning, friendship slowly developed into love. But if they were to get married, Hawthorne needed more money than he was likely to earn by

Above *Nathaniel Hawthorne, age 36, in a portrait painted in 1840 by Charles Osgood. By this time Hawthorne was engaged to Sophia and had successfully published a number of stories and tales to considerable literary acclaim, but little financial reward.*

writing. Sophia's sister, Elizabeth, wrote letters to various influential people on his behalf, and in November 1838 he was appointed to the Boston Custom House. This gave him a reasonable salary. Meanwhile, Nathaniel and Sophia exchanged warm and intimate letters. Nathaniel wrote to Sophia:

"You only have revealed me to myself, for without your aid my best knowledge of myself would have been merely to know my own shadow—to watch it flickering on the wall, and mistake its fantasies for my own real actions. Do you comprehend what you have done for me?"

They became secretly engaged in about April 1839. Sophia's letter, printed here, was written at the end of that year. Both sensible and hopeful, she shared with him her inclination to link ordinary things and events—such as the matches (*"allumettes"*) and country walk mentioned in the letter—with the eternal.

Left *Nathaniel's inscription to Sophia written inside the presentation copy he gave her in 1838 of his famous book* Twice Told Tales (*published in 1837*), *a collection of stories full of psychological and moral insight.*

Finding the money to marry, however, remained a problem. Nathaniel invested his Boston earnings in a back-to-the-soil utopian scheme at Brook Farm, West Roxbury, Massachusetts, an agricultural cooperative run in accordance with the ideas of the French social reformer, Charles Fourier. But the experiment failed and he lost his money. Nevertheless, Sophia and Nathaniel decided they would not wait any longer. They married on July 9, 1842. For the next three-and-a-half years they lived in the Old Manse at Concord, in what was probably the most idyllic time of their 22-year marriage. In his diary, the *American Notebooks*, he wrote:

"We seem to have been translated to the other state of being, without having passed through death."

They lived on what they grew in the garden, and savored one another's company and the quiet of the country. Hawthorne wrote:

"It is usually supposed that the cares of life come with matrimony but I seem to have cast off all cares….My chief anxiety consists in watching the prosperity of my vegetables."

❧ *T h e   L o v e r s* ❧

SOPHIA AMELIA PEABODY
(1809–71)
was born in Salem, Massachusetts, in 1809, the youngest of three sisters. She and her sisters Elizabeth and Mary were educated by their mother at her small private school. Elizabeth later became a famous pioneer of kindergarten education. Sophia, though troubled by ill health for much of her life, was a good painter and a skillful copyist. From 1833–35 she lived in Cuba, in the hope that the climate might there improve her health. She also wrote articles that were published in American journals. After her marriage to Nathaniel Hawthorne she proved a supportive and resourceful wife, at one time keeping the family finances afloat by making lampshades. They had three children: Una, Julian, and Rose.

NATHANIEL HAWTHORNE
(1804–64),
American novelist and short story writer, was born in Salem, Massachusetts. His father died when he was four. He and his sisters were educated by his uncle, and he then attended Bowdoin College in Maine. By 1842 he had a growing reputation as a short story writer but little income. In a period of unemployment between work for the customs service he wrote *The Scarlet Letter* (1850), at once hailed as a masterpiece. The novel that followed, *The House of the Seven Gables*, the story of a curse eventually lifted by love, solidified his reputation as a fine writer. From 1853–57 he served in England as American consul in Liverpool, and then visited Italy with his family. They returned to New England, where Hawthorne died at age 60.

Right and inset *The Old Manse in Concord, Massachusetts, the Hawthorne's home from 1842 to 1845. In April 1843 they incised on a windowpane: "Man's accidents are God's purposes/ Sophia A. Hawthorne 1843"; "Nath Hawthorne/This is his study/ 1843"; and "The smallest twig/Leans clear against the sky. Composed by my wife, and written with her dia-/mond."*

It was during this time that Hawthorne wrote his novel *Mosses from an Old Manse*. In March 1844, their first child, Una, was born, and Nathaniel welcomed the new responsibility:

"I have business on earth now, and must look about me for the means of doing it."

The Hawthornes moved back to Salem from Boston in 1845, then to Lenox in 1850. Two more children arrived: Julian in 1846 and Rose in 1851. Sophia delighted in the children, while Nathaniel—a loving and playful father—maintained his edge of humor.

"The children…seem very good and beautiful at this distance,"

he wrote one time from New York.

Hawthorne's triumph as a writer came in 1849 when, after six months' intensive work, he completed *The Scarlet Letter*, an exploration of tragic love in the harsh Puritan New England past. When he read it to Sophia, his voice breaking with emotion,

"It broke her heart and sent her to bed with a grievous headache, which I look upon as a triumphant success."

After writing a biography of his friend Franklin Pierce, who became president in 1852, Nathaniel was given a consulship in Liverpool, England, where the family lived from 1853 to 1860. With their financial difficulties greatly reduced, the family continued to thrive. On a visit to Italy 10 years later, the children's governess, Ada Shepard, described it as,

"the happiest home-circle I have ever seen."

Hawthorne died in 1864, after a life made full by his years with Sophia, who wrote:

"God has turned for me the silver lining and for me the darkest cloud has broken into ten thousand singing birds."

The marriage of Nathaniel and Sophia has been described as "a classic of American marital idylls." In spite of financial hardship and other difficulties, their delight in one another never faded. They shared a spiritual outlook on life, and perhaps this, above all, accounts for the deep joy they brought each other during their long marriage.

Elizabeth Barrett to Robert Browning

Above *Elizabeth Barrett with her dog Flush, in a sketch by her brother Alfred in 1840.*

January 10, 1846

Do you know, when you have told me to think of you, I have been feeling ashamed of thinking of you so much, of thinking of only you—which is too much, perhaps. Shall I tell you? It seems to me, to myself, that no man was ever before to any woman what you are to me—the fulness must be in proportion, you know, to the vacancy…and only I know what was behind—the long wilderness without the blossoming rose…and the capacity for happiness, like a black gaping hole, before this silver flooding. Is it wonderful that I should stand as in a dream, and disbelieve—not you—but my own fate? Was ever any one taken suddenly from a lampless dungeon and placed upon the pinnacle of a mountain, without the head turning round and the heart turning faint, as mine do? And you love me more, you say?—Shall I thank you or God? Both,—indeed—and there is no possible return from me to either of you! I thank you as the unworthy may…and as we all thank God. How shall I ever prove what my heart is to you? How will you ever see it as I feel it? I ask myself in vain.

Have so much faith in me, my only beloved, as to use me simply for your own advantage and happiness, and to your own ends without a thought of any others—that is all I could ask you without any disquiet as to the granting of it—May God bless you!—

Your

B.A.

Below *Robert always brought fresh flowers to Elizabeth's room. Her letter of January 10 is also shown.*

On January 10, 1845, a struggling 32-year-old writer, Robert Browning, wrote to congratulate the English poet Elizabeth Barrett on her latest book of poems, which included in it a tribute to his own verse. He wrote enthusiastically,

"I love your verses."

Near the end of his letter, he added

"and I love you too."

His declaration was sincere, and the more extraordinary in that he made it to a woman whom he had never met. A back injury had made Elizabeth a semi-invalid 24 years earlier. The death of her favorite brother, Edward (known as Bro)—who drowned at sea in a mysterious boating accident in 1840—added to her sorrow. She scarcely moved from the sofa on which she spent her housebound days in London's Wimpole Street, exacerbating her ill health with the painkiller opium. She was watched over by her widowed father, Edward Barrett, a sternly loving, but possessive man. To him, Elizabeth was,

"the purest woman he ever knew,"

by which, as she told Robert, he meant she had not

"troubled him with the iniquity of love affairs, or any impropriety of seeming to think about being married."

Little did Robert know at the time that his letter to his fellow poet ended Mr. Barrett's comfortable circumstance with his daughter once and for all.

Above *Robert Browning at age 43, painted by Dante Gabriel Rossetti in 1855. That year Browning published* Men and Women, *a collection of 51 poems. Disappointed by its reception, he spent the next six years looking after his adored wife, Elizabeth.*

Browning's first impulsive letter to Elizabeth was written as one poet to another. His only substantial knowledge of her was surmised from having read and greatly admired her poems. He could "love" her only as the "great soul" he believed her words revealed. In later years his subtle, ironic genius would flower too and be recognized, but at this stage, the 38-year-old Elizabeth was the greater in both reputation and achievement. Yet, in response to his first letter to her, she wrote back excitedly, asking to take up his offer to give advice on her work,

"as a fellow-craftsman should."

She encouraged him to:

"tell me of such faults as rise to the surface and strike you as important,"

believing he had much he could teach her. As the two poets "talked on paper," "the honor of acquaintance" quickly developed into "the delight of friendship." Nothing pleased her more than to have found a kindred spirit who understood what she was trying to achieve in her poetry. And in her fourth letter to him—more relaxed in tone than the previous letters she had

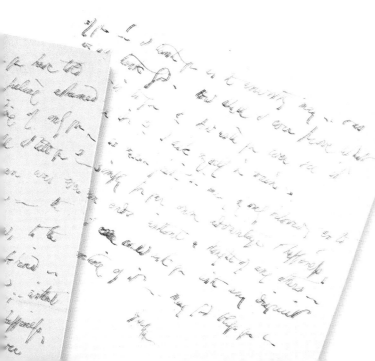

written him—she told him that she wanted to know everything about him, by what she described as,

"refracted lights as well as direct ones."

Fear that he would not like her when he met her made her put off the occasion for as long as possible, but with Robert's gentle encouragement she finally relented. When they met for the first time in May 1845, they already knew a good deal about each other. To the diminutive Elizabeth lying on her sofa, her pale face framed by thick black ringlets, Robert seemed to have

"drunken the cup of life full…"

while she had

"lived only inwardly. Books and dreams were what I lived in."

This was not quite true. Certainly Browning had seen more places and lived more in the world, but he too was sheltered. Like Elizabeth he was largely self-educated, reading from childhood in his father's 6,000-volume library. Like her he still lived at home. Like her he had never had to earn a living and could dedicate himself entirely to writing poetry. But Elizabeth, who had

"beheld no great mountain or river,"

felt the need to escape from seclusion into experience, and Robert was her lifeline, the more so because he was in love. For her, this new-found love was nothing more than a miracle,

"a silver flooding,"

as she wrote in the letter extracted here, exactly one year after she had received his first letter to her. For Browning, she was the miracle. Prior to their first meeting he had never kept a journal, but now he recorded the date and length of every visit,

Below The title page of Elizabeth's copy of her book Poems (1844). At some point she crossed out her surname "Barrett" and substituted "Browning."

Above The Barrett home at 50 Wimpole Street, London, as it would have been in the 1840's. Before her secret flight to Italy with Robert, Elizabeth rarely left her third-floor room here.

"the number of minutes you have given me"

as well as his feelings:

"love was to feel you in my very heart and hold you there for ever, through all chance and earthly changes."

Over the course of two years they exchanged some 600 letters. Such delight between well-suited people should naturally and simply have led to marriage. But the implacable Mr. Barrett only allowed "the poet" to visit because he did not see him as a threat

Below Robert and Elizabeth's marriage certificate, dated September 12, 1846.

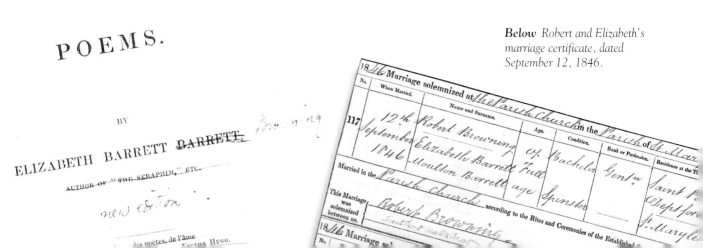

POEMS.

BY

ELIZABETH BARRETT ~~BARRETT~~ Browning

AUTHOR OF "THE SERAPHIM," ETC.

to his household. Elizabeth seemed to be getting better, venturing outside, as she said,

> "scarcely an invalid."

On May 12, 1846, she wrote excitedly to Robert,

> "Look what is inside this letter—look! It is a laburnum flower,"

a return for all the flowers he had brought to brighten her invalid's drawing room. She had picked it herself, stopping the carriage, putting

> "both my feet on the grass…which was the strangest feeling!"

In one letter, she wrote full of hope, saying,

> "Dearest, we shall walk together under the trees some day."

Throughout the summer of 1846 Elizabeth knew she could only marry against her father's will. She agonized over the wound she would inflict on him and what she feared would be the inevitable loss of his love. The last thing she wanted was to hurt him. After all, she wrote,

> "He is not stone…His hand would not lie so heavily without a pulse in it."

She struggled too with the immense effort of will needed to marry and elope to the chosen country, Italy, which would provide the right climate for an invalid with incipient lung trouble. Browning, meanwhile, made all the arrangements, which were kept secret from Elizabeth's father.

On September 12, 1846, they were married at St. Marylebone church, not far from Elizabeth's home. Robert carefully recorded it in his journal as their 91st meeting. After the service they went back to their separate homes to make final preparations to leave the country, Elizabeth wondering how she could ever write,

> "Papa I am married; I hope you will not be too displeased,"

On September 20 Robert, Elizabeth, Wilson her faithful servant, and Flush the dog landed in France. Elizabeth wrote:

> "But love me for love's sake, that evermore
> Thou mayst love on, through love's eternity."

Mr. Barrett never spoke or wrote to his daughter again and died in 1857 without forgiving her. The two poets lived happily together for 15 years, alternating between Florence, Rome, London, and Paris. They were separated from each other only when Elizabeth died, cradled in Robert's arms.

Above *Elizabeth's sketch of a fig tree, made in Siena in 1860. Robert added, "Drawn the last time she ever sat under it. We left the next day. R.B." Elizabeth died the following June, in Florence.*

❧ *The Lovers* ❧

ELIZABETH MOULTON BARRETT
(1806–61),
poet, was born near Durham, England, eldest of a family of 12 children, and grew up in the countryside. In 1838 the Barretts moved to 50 Wimpole Street, London. By the time Robert Browning began to correspond with her in 1845, she was an established poet. Four years after their runaway marriage, she wrote her most famous love poems, *Sonnets from the Portuguese*. The couple settled in Florence, where their son, Robert Wiedemann Barrett (known as Pen for short), was born in 1849. Elizabeth was then 43. She had a huge popular success with *Aurora Leigh* (1857), a love story in verse. Her always delicate health gradually became worse; she died on June 29, 1861, and is buried in Florence.

ROBERT BROWNING
(1812–89),
a great Victorian poet, was born in London, the son of a clerk in the Bank of England, and educated by his father, who paid for the printing of his first poems. His early works, mostly verse plays, were little read and less understood. *Men and Women* (1855), his first collection of dramatic lyrics, sold few copies and the disappointed Browning abandoned writing to care for his adored wife. After her death he turned again to poetry; *Dramatis Personae* (1864) was a success and was followed by his greatest work, *The Ring and the Book* (1868–69), which established him as a literary giant, although his many succeeding books never sold as well as Elizabeth's. He died in Venice in the winter of 1889 and is buried in Westminster Abbey.

Anton Chekhov to Olga Knipper

September 1, 1902
Yalta

My dear, my own,

Once again I have had a strange letter from you. Once again you hurl all sorts of accusations at my head. Who has told you that I don't want to go back to Moscow, that I have gone away for good and am not coming back this autumn? Didn't I write to you in plain Russian, that I would definitely be coming back in September and would live with you till December. Well, didn't I? You accuse me of not being frank, yet you forget everything I write or say to you. And I simply can't imagine what I am to do with my wife, or how I should write to her.

You write that you tremble when you read my letters, that it is time for us to part, that there is something you don't understand in all this. It strikes me, my darling, that neither I nor you are to blame for all this muddle, but someone else with whom you have been talking....You write that I am capable of living beside you and always being silent, that I only want you as an agreeable woman and that as a human being you are isolated and a stranger to me. My sweet, good darling, you are my wife, when are you finally going to understand that? You are the person nearest and dearest to me. I have loved you infinitely and I love you still and you go writing about being an agreeable woman, lonely and a stranger to me....Well then, have it your own way if you must!

I am better, but I've been coughing violently. There hasn't been any rain, and it's hot....

Write and tell me what you're doing, what parts you are playing, which new ones you're rehearsing. You are not lazy like your husband, are you?...I love you more than ever and as a husband I have been blameless. Why can't you finally understand that my joy, my scribble-scrabble?

Good-bye for the present, keep well and cheerful. Write to me every day without fail. I kiss you and hug you, my puppet.

Your A

3820. О. Л. КНИППЕР-ЧЕХОВОЙ
1 сентября 1902 г. Ялта.
тября.
ая моя, родная, опять я получил от тебя странное
. Опять ты взваливаешь на мою башку разные раз-
Кто тебе сказал, что я не хочу вернуться в Москву,
уехал совсем и уже не вернусь этой осенью? Ведь я же
тебе, писал ясно, русским языком, что я приеду не-
нно в сентябре и буду жить вместе с тобой до декабря.
е не писал? Ты обвиняешь меня в неоткровенности,
жду тем ты забываешь всё, что я говорю тебе или пишу.
осто не придумаю, что мне делать с моей супругой, как
ать ей. Ты пишешь, что тебя дрожь пробирает при чте-
моих писем, что нам пора разлучаться, что ты чего-то
понимаешь во всем... Мне кажется, дуся моя, что во всей
й каше виноват не я и не ты, а кто-то другой, с кем ты
говорила. В тебя вложено недоверие к моим словам,
моим движениям, всё тебе кажется подозрительным –
уж тут я ничего не могу поделать, не могу и не могу. И ра-
уверять тебя и переубеждать не стану, ибо бесполезно.
Ты пишешь, что я способен жить около тебя и все мол-
чать, что нужна ты мне только как приятная женщина
и что ты сама как человек живешь чуждой мне и одинокой... Дуся моя милая, хорошая, ведь ты моя жена, пойми
это наконец! Ты самый близкий и дорогой мне человек,
я тебя любил безгранично и люблю, а ты расписываешься
«приятной» женщиной, чуждой мне и одинокой... Ну, да
бог с тобой, как хочешь.
Здоровье мое лучше, но кашляю я неистово. Дождей
нет, жарко. Маша уезжает 4-го, будет в Москве 6-го. Ты
пишешь, что я покажу Маше твое письмо; спасибо за до-
верие. Кстати сказать, Маша решительно ни в чем не
виновата, в этом ты рано или поздно убедишься.
Начал читать пьесу Найденова. Не нравится мне. Не
хочется дочитывать до конца. Когда переедешь в Москву,
то телеграфируй. Надоело писать чужие адресы. Удочку
мою не забудь, заверни удилище в бумагу. Будь весела, не
... по крайней мере делай вид, что ты весела.
... рассказывала много, но неин-
... болела, кто около тебя

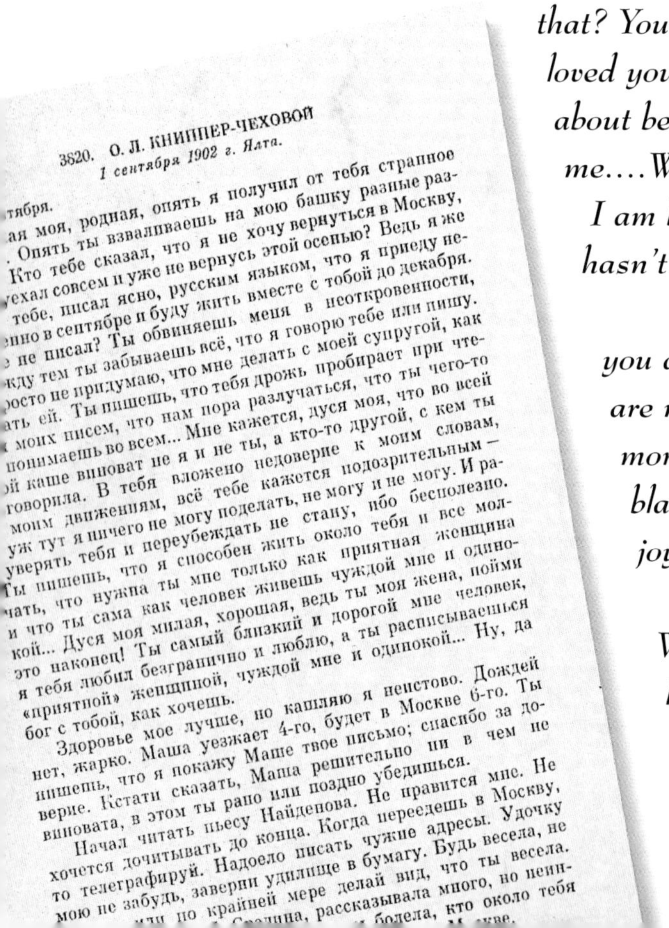

The Russian playwright, Anton Chekhov, met the actress Olga Knipper for the first time on September 9, 1898, during rehearsals for his play *The Seagull*. He was 38 and she was 10 years younger. Shortly after their meeting, Chekhov, who had advanced tuberculosis, went south from Moscow to Yalta in the Crimea for the good of his health. He took with him memories of Olga's voice, her nobility and warmth. He told a friend that if he had stayed on in Moscow he would have fallen in love. Olga, like the rest of the company, found Chekhov's charm overwhelming. Soon a correspondence developed between them, Anton relying on Olga's letters to keep him in touch with the wider world. Courtship and marriage followed, characterized by brief meetings and long separations; but their relationship, founded on love, was sound. Their letters to each other were a source of joy and consolation, through illness and separation.

Chekhov, descended from serfs and trained as a doctor, had supported his family since 1879. As well as tending the sick, he busied himself visiting schools and establishing libraries. But Chekhov earned most of his income selling comic stories to magazines. Gradually he raised his literary sights, and by the time he met Olga he had a growing reputation as writer and dramatist.

Family necessity brought Olga to the theater too. When her apparently well-off father died in 1894, he left his family heavily in debt. To earn a living Olga gave music lessons. In 1895 she entered drama school, and three years later joined the new Moscow Art Theater. When Anton met her—a tall and elegant woman, with dark-brown hair, vivid eyes, and an expressive face—she and the company were about to take Moscow by storm with a vibrant interpretation

Above *Olga Knipper, photographed in 1899. When Chekhov saw her he thought "There's a demon lurking behind your modest expression of quiet sadness."*

of *The Seagull*. They brilliantly revealed the passion he concealed beneath the quietly comic surfaces of Russian life. This same wry sense of humor sustained the sensitive writer throughout the years that he suffered from the debilitating symptoms of tuberculosis.

In May 1899, with spring in full flower, Chekhov invited Olga to his mother's home in the country. In her memoirs Olga recalled happily,

"We had three days filled with a sense of anticipation, with joy and sun."

Over the summer they corresponded, Chekhov addressing her with,

"Greetings, last page of my life, great actress of the Russian land."

Their relationship took a decisive turn in August, when Olga, who was staying with family friends in Yalta, traveled back to Moscow with Anton. Part of the way took them by carriage through the beautiful Kokkoz Valley. There they came to some kind of "agreement." Anton later wrote to Olga saying how he scarcely went into his beautiful Yalta garden, but sat indoors and thought of her, remembering their journey together. He wrote,

"I warmly press and kiss your hand. Be well, merry, happy, work, skip about, be enthusiastic, sing and, if possible, don't forget the retired author, your devout admirer. A. Chekhov."

Olga became his mistress in the summer of 1899, flirtation turning to a deep and sincere love. Their life was full of partings, and they were separated for long stretches. Chekhov lived in warm, dull Yalta, while Olga continued her career in glamorous but cold Moscow. However, that summer Chekhov, partly through fear and partly out of consideration, was slow to propose. On August 13, Olga complained to Chekhov's devoted sister, Masha,

"Can anyone come to a decision with him?"

The following month, on September 27, Chekhov wrote defending himself,

> *"If we're not together now, it's not my fault or yours, but that of the devil who implanted the bacilli in me and the love of art in you."*

There were many things to consider. How would marriage to Anton in far-off Yalta affect Olga's acting career? What about Masha, who had turned down offers of marriage to look after him? Would the strain of marriage, as Masha believed, be too much for Anton? Chekhov himself had an inner core of loneliness, made worse by his illness, that made him afraid of committing himself to another person. Sometimes his good-humored self-sufficiency seemed to Olga like indifference.

Eventually, however, he gave in to pressure, and they married, secretly and happily, on May 25, 1901, in Moscow. To avoid any fuss or sentimentality, Anton invited most of their friends and relatives to a dinner in Moscow, which he and Olga deliberately failed to attend. Even Masha and her mother first heard the news by telegram. In his plays and prose, Chekhov had often portrayed marriages as either comic or unhappy. Perhaps he was embarrassed to have succumbed at last, after so many years of flirtations and short affairs. But in December 1902 he had one regret; he wrote,

> *"We have one fault in common, we married each other too late."*

After the wedding their long separations continued. A child might have kept them together, but Olga miscarried. Then, inevitably, Chekhov's illness worsened and on July 1, 1904, he died. Olga was at his bedside. At the last, he was given champagne. Glass in hand, he smiled and said,

> *"It's a long while since I've drunk champagne."*

He drank it, turned on his side and died moments later. A huge black moth suddenly flew in through the open window, batted wildly against the lamp, and then found its way out, leaving silence. Olga later consoled herself with the recollection:

> *"There was only beauty, peace and the grandeur of death."*

Above *Anton Chekhov, photographed in the garden of his villa at Yalta in 1901, the year he and Olga married.*

Right *The title page of Chekhov's drama* Three Sisters *(published in 1902), showing Olga (center) as Masha. This was one of a series of roles written with Olga in mind.*

The Lovers

ANTON PAVLOVICH CHEKHOV
(1860–1904)
was well educated in the classics and
graduated as a doctor in 1884. After
his father, a grocer, went bankrupt,
Chekhov provided financial support
for his large family by writing popular
comic sketches for humorous journals. From 1888 his work became
more serious—though with an
underlying humor—and in the 16
years before his death he published
more than 50 stories in leading literary journals. But his reputation as a
major Russian writer rests on his
plays: *The Seagull (1896)*, *Uncle
Vanya (1900)*, *The Three Sisters
(1901)*, and *The Cherry Orchard
(1904)*. Chekhov valued political
and artistic freedom highly. A
religious skeptic, he was drawn to an
ascetic lifestyle. He died in Germany
in 1904 from tuberculosis that had
made him an invalid for many years.

OLGA LEONARDOVNA KNIPPER
(1869–1959)
was the daughter of an engineer of
German descent. She was educated
in music, drawing, and foreign languages. After the death of her father
left the family in debt, she went to
drama school, later joining the
Moscow Art Theater where she
worked under Konstantin
Stanislavsky. She performed in all
the Moscow Art Theater's original
productions of Chekhov's plays, to
great acclaim. In 1901 she married
Chekhov. They were often separated
during their marriage, and letters
played an important part in their
relationship; touchingly Olga continued to write to Anton after his death
in 1904. She also continued her brilliant acting career, touring Europe
from 1919 to 1922, and the United
States from 1923 to 1924. In 1943
she performed in the Moscow Art
Theater's 300th performance of *The
Cherry Orchard*. Olga died at age 89.

Left *The villa at Yalta where
Chekhov spent his last years. His
sister Maria planted the cypress tree
(far left) on the day of his death.*

Robert Peary to his wife, Jo

August 17, 1908
S.S. Roosevelt,

Above *Josephine Diebitsch Peary,
photographed in arctic furs.*

My Darling:

Am nearly through with my writing. Am brain weary with the thousand and one imperative details and things to think of. Everything thus far has gone well, too well I am afraid, and I am (solely on general principles) somewhat suspicious of the future.

The ship is in better shape than before; the party and crew are apparently harmonious; I have 21 Eskimo men (against 23 last time) but the total of men women and children is only 50 as against 67 before owing to a more careful selection as to children....

I have landed supplies here, and leave two men ostensibly on behalf of Cook. As a matter of fact I have established here the sub-base which last I established at Victoria Head, as a precaution in event of loss of the Roosevelt either going up this fall or coming down next summer.

In some respects this is an advantage as on leaving here there is nothing to delay me or keep me from taking either side of the Channel going up. The conditions give me entire control of the situation....

You have been with me constantly, sweetheart. At Kangerdlooksoah I looked repeatedly at Ptarmigan Island and thought of the time we camped there. At Nuuatoksoah I landed where we were. And on the 11th we passed the mouth of Bowdoin Bay in brilliant weather, and as long as I could I kept my eyes on Anniversary Lodge. We have been great chums dear.

Tell Marie to remember what I told her, tell "Mister Man" [Robert Peary, Jr.] to remember "straight and strong and clean and honest," obey orders, and never forget that Daddy put "Mut" in his charge till he himself comes back to take her.

In fancy I kiss your dear eyes and lips and cheeks sweetheart; and dream of you and my children, and my home till I come again.

Kiss my babies for me.

Aufwiedersehen. Love, Love, Love.

Your Bert

P.S. August 18, 9 a.m. ...Tell Marie that her fir pillow perfumes me to sleep.

The American Arctic explorer Robert Peary married Josephine Diebitsch on August 11, 1888. He was a handsome, powerful man with one driving ambition, to be the first man to stand at the top of the world, the North Pole. In the years of their marriage, as his ambition became obsession, Josephine stood by him, accepting years of anxious waiting. Peary wrote her the letter extracted here as he prepared his final assault on his "destiny." Eight months later, and 23 years after he had first formed the idea, he wrote excitedly in his diary,

> *"The Pole at last!!!...I wish Jo could be here with me to share my feelings."*

Early in their marriage Jo was determined not to be left at home while her husband went away for months at a time, and went with Peary in 1891 to the Arctic to face the same dangers that he faced. Elegant and fastidious, she was an unlikely member of a dangerous expedition, but she was loyal, brave, and completely devoted to her husband. Two pictures remained fixed in his mind from that expedition. One was their first night ashore in Greenland, when they camped in a little

> *"tent—which the furious wind threatened every moment to carry away bodily—she watched by my side as I lay a helpless cripple with a broken leg."*

The other vivid picture was from a month or two later,

> *"...this same woman sat for an hour beside me in the stern of a boat, calmly reloading our empty firearms while a herd of infuriated walrus thrust their savage heads with gleaming tusks and bloodshot eyes out of the water so that she could have touched them with her hand."*

Right *Robert Peary on board the S.S. Roosevelt during the 1908–09 expedition which he claimed reached the North Pole. The 50-strong Inuit team of guides helped to make his suit of animal skins.*

On a subsequent expedition in September 1893, Jo gave birth to their first child, Marie Ahnighito, at Anniversary Lodge, their new expedition base on Bowdoin Bay, Inglefield Gulf in northwestern Greenland. No white child, let alone a newborn baby, had ever been seen so far north, and Inuits from miles around came to see the,

> *"little blue-eyed snowflake,"*

to satisfy themselves by actual touch that she was really a creature of warm flesh and blood, and not of snow, as they had at first believed.

Those expeditions and the ones that followed it were all failures, beset by misfortunes and appalling weather conditions. On August 28, 1894, in a particularly depressed mood, he wrote to Jo:

> *"Never have I felt more lonely than tonight, never if God grants me to take you in my arms again will I leave you for so long again....I have lost my sanguine hope....I think at times perhaps I have lost you."*

But he had not lost her. How much he depended on her shows in a letter dated August 27, 1899, after Jo had written telling him of the birth of their second child, a daughter named Francine. He wrote back:

> *"Never was a man more fortunate in his wife than I, never a*

Below *The diary entry for April 6, 1909, backing Peary's claim to success. Later explorers questioned this evidence, wondering why the entry was on a loose sheet inserted among other blank pages.*

Above *Peary and Jo in summer 1901, briefly reunited on the Arctic island of Ellesmere after a three-year separation.*

Right *Josephine Peary Island, near Inglefield Gulf, Greenland. It was partly explored by her husband in 1892, 1895, and again in 1900.*

wife more loving, tender, delicious, yet with it all, clear and level headed. Your letter was like an exquisite soft warm breeze of spring in this lonely desert....You are right dear, life is slipping away.... More than once I have taken myself to task for my folly in leaving such a wife and baby (babies now) for this work. But there is something beyond me, something outside of me, which impels me irresistibly to the work. I shall certainly come back to you, then hand in hand we will meet the days and years until the end comes."

In a letter dated January 23, 1901, Jo wrote back, no longer able to contain her anxiety,

"You must take care of yourself. Sometimes I think you are a physical wreck, if this is so, come home and let Marie and me love you and nurse you.... Oh Bert, Bert. I want you so much. Life is slipping away so fast—pretty soon all will be over."

Peary received this together with an earlier letter, dated March 1900. Jo had borne, alone, the death of seven-month-old Francine. To compound this grief,

she had heard at the same time that Peary had been crippled by frostbite. She had written,

"I shall never feel quite the same again, part of me is in the little grave...the news of your terrible suffering nearly prostrated me but you know I am strong and can bear and bear....Oh Sweetheart, husband, together we could have shared it but alone it was almost too much."

On May 6, 1901, Peary returned to his wife and daughter after an absence of three years. He set out again in 1905, and although this renewed effort to reach the Pole ended in a new record Farthest North, his team were forced to turn back at a latitude of 87° 06'. In spite of the hardships of the earlier expeditions, Peary was still obsessed with reaching the Pole. On July 17, 1908, he set out for one last attempt. His letter, extracted here, recalls Jo's visit to the Arctic and is full of love for their children, Marie and Robert Jr., "Mister Man," born in September 1903. It was the prelude to a soured success.

"The Pole at last!!!"

ROBERT PEARY
(1856–1920)
was born in Cresson, Pennsylvania. At 25, he joined the navy, which gave him leave of absence for Arctic exploration. He made his first expedition to Greenland in 1886 with his lifelong associate Matthew Henson; on his second expedition in 1891 he discovered Independence Fjord and brought back evidence of Greenland being an island. Attempts to reach the North Pole in 1900, 1902, and 1905 all ended in failure. Finally, in 1909 he announced to the world that he had succeeded. That same year his rival Dr. Frederick Cook claimed to have reached the Pole a year earlier. Cook's claim was dismissed, and Peary's was eventually accepted, in spite of widespread doubt. He retired as a rear admiral in 1911, and lived with his family on Eagle Island off the coast of Maine until his death nine years later.

JOSEPHINE DIEBITSCH
(1863–1955)
was born in Washington D.C., the daughter of a Prussian father and a Saxon mother. She met Robert in 1882 when he was an ambitious young naval officer. He proposed to her in 1887 as he was preparing for an expedition to Nicaragua, and the couple married on his return, the following year. In 1891 Jo went with her husband on his first trip to Greenland, becoming the first white woman to have traveled so far north. Six months pregnant, she insisted on going with him again in 1893 and gave birth to their first child, Marie, in Greenland. She went again in 1897 and in 1900, when their ship was ice-bound for the winter. After this Jo stayed at home, raising funds for Robert's expeditions and enduring long separations, often for two or three years at a time. The *National Geographic Society* awarded her its Gold Medal in 1955.

Left The Peary family, photographed after Robert's retirement to Eagle Island ("the Sanctuary") off the coast of Maine. With Robert and Josephine are Marie Ahnighito Peary, born at Anniversary Lodge, Greenland, in 1893 and Robert Peary Jr. ("Mister Man"), born in 1903.

1911, that thanked him for his services and placed him on the retirement pay of a rear admiral. However, many influential people were unconvinced that he had achieved his goal. Until this time, a gentleman explorer's word had been sufficient, and Peary had never thought he would have to produce unimpeachable proofs. (The debate continued into the 1980's, when an investigation suggested that he may have been 30–60 miles short of the Pole.) He was honored worldwide but, as Jo wrote, this final challenge hurt more than all the hardships he endured in the Arctic. In the end, the real consolation for a life of obsessed courage was, as it always had been, Jo's love, steadfast through years of separation.

But was it? On his return, Peary's sketchy and incomplete calculations of his team's final position were called into question. The daily distances he claimed seemed impossible; and there were blank pages in the record. After a two-year wrangle his claim seemed to be vindicated by a bill passed through Congress in

Winston Churchill to his wife, Clementine

January 23, 1935

My darling Clemmie,

In your letter from Madras you wrote some words vy dear to me, about my having enriched yr life. I cannot tell you what pleasure this gave me, because I always feel so overwhelmingly in yr debt, if there can be accounts in love. It was sweet of you to write this to me, and I hope and pray I shall be able to make you happy and secure during my remaining years, and cherish you my darling one as you deserve, and leave you in comfort when my race is run. What it has been to me to live all these years in yr heart and companionship no phrases can convey. Time passes swiftly, but is it not joyous to see how great and growing is the treasure we have gathered together, amid the storms and stresses of so many eventful and to millions tragic and terrible years?…

Your loving husband,

Early in January 1935 50-year-old Clementine Churchill—for many years the devoted wife of Winston Spencer Churchill, one of England's most prominent politicians—was making the long sea voyage from England to Indonesia. On New Year's Day, 1935, she wrote to her husband from a stop in India,

"Oh my Darling, I'm thinking so much of you and how you have enriched my life. I have loved you very much but I wish I had been a more amusing wife to you. How nice it would be if we were both young again."

Winston's reply, reprinted here, reflected a devotion that had not dimmed in 27 years of marriage. Their partnership, in fact, survived for another 30 years, weathering all the stresses and strains that came from lives led on the world stage.

Churchill first met beautiful 19-year-old Clementine Hozier at a ball in London in 1904. He was 30 and already launched into the adventurous life of a soldier, journalist, and politician. Four years passed before their next meeting in March 1908, when the two were irrevocably drawn to each other. As he wrote to her the following month,

"What a comfort and pleasure it was to me to meet a girl with so much intellectual quality and such strong reserves of noble sentiment."

Clementine found Churchill's charm and charisma irresistible too. Love blossomed, and on August 10, 1908, he proposed to her in the gardens of his birthplace, Blenheim Palace, in Oxfordshire. They were soon exchanging notes breathless with love. In one, Churchill wrote:

"My dearest, I hope you slept like a stone…. The purpose of this

Above *Studied elegance characterizes this portrait of Clementine Churchill, taken by the famed society photographer Cecil Beaton in New York in 1932. She was in America accompanying Winston on a nationwide lecture tour.*

letter is also to send you heaps of love and four kisses X X X X."

Her reply to this note ended joyfully,

"Je t'aime passionement [sic]—feel less shy in French."

Another letter from Clementine to Winston written that August ended with the words,

"Goodbye my darling. I feel there is no room for anyone but you in my heart—you fill every corner."

Just one month after their engagement, Winston and Clementine were married at St. Margaret's Church, Westminster. The ceremony was followed by a honeymoon in Italy. On their return, Churchill plunged into politics as a member of the reforming Liberal government. Their lifetime of corresponding began at this period. Clementine, expecting their first child, stayed at Blenheim while Winston remained in London, near Parliament.

In their letters, Clementine referred to herself as "Kat" or "Cat"; Winston was "Pug" or later "Pig," and even the children received pet names. The letters

Left *Winston at his desk in Chartwell, the Churchills' country house in Kent, southeast England, for over 40 years. It was here that he did most of his writing—books and articles—and where he sought refuge from the heavy demands of a life devoted to politics.*

were invariably decorated with a drawing of a cat, pig, or pug dog. Subjects ranged widely, from the concerns of home to major political events. To Winston, Clementine was a beacon of sanity. He ended a letter that he sent her in April 1909 with the affectionate words,

> *"Thus the world wages—good, bad and indifferent…and only my sweet Pussy cat remains a constant darling…"*

He worried about her health. After the birth of their first child in July 1909, he urged,

> *"…do try to gather your strength….Remember my two rules—No walk of more than 1/2 a mile; no risk of catching cold….I do so want your life to be a full and sweet one."*

After the arrival in 1911 of their second child, Randolph (named after his grandfather), she wrote,

> *"My sweet beloved Winston, I am so happy with you my Dear. You have so transformed my life that I can hardly remember what it felt like three years ago before I knew you."*

But in a postscript she gently chided,

> *"Please be a good Pug and not destroy the good of your little open air holiday by smoking too many fat cigars."*

In 1915, during World War I, Churchill went to France to gain experience of trench warfare. Foreboding filled her letter in November of that year:

> *"…for seven years you have filled my whole life and now I feel more than half my life has vanished across the channel…I feel you are receding into the fog and mud of Flanders…"*

He continued to rely on her support while he was abroad. Taking strength from her, he wrote,

> *"Show complete confidence in our fortunes. Hold your head vy high. You always do."*

Throughout the vicissitudes of his career, Churchill always believed in his destiny. At the end of 1915, during World War I, he wrote,

> *"My conviction that the greatest of my work is still to come is strong within me…"*

Clementine supported his belief, and he recognized just how much he needed her. On their eleventh wedding anniversary in September 1919, he wrote:

> *"…it is a rock of comfort to have your love and companionship at my side."*

Above *Clementine often decorated her letters to Winston with a sketch of a cat. He, in turn, drew pigs (see **below far right**). The animals represented their pet names for each other. She was "Kat," he "Pig" (or at other times "Pug").*

Right *Winston's painting of Chartwell Manor under a covering of snow, done in the mid-1930's. Winston was an enthusiastic and talented amateur painter. He even set up a studio in Chartwell's grounds.*

Below *Sharing the grimness of the hour, Winston and Clementine set out on a tour to visit the bomb-damaged streets of east London during September 1940, when the city was hit by the German "blitz." The picture was one of the Churchill family's best-loved pictures of the couple.*

❦ *The Lovers* ❦

WINSTON SPENCER CHURCHILL
(1874–1965)
was born at Blenheim Palace in Oxfordshire, son of Lord Randolph Churchill and Jennie Jerome. Educated at Harrow, he served in the army in India and Sudan, then went to South Africa as a war correspondent to cover the Boer War. In 1904 he joined the Liberal Party (returning to the Conservatives 20 years later); and in 1908 married Clementine Hozier. Churchill held many high offices of state, including home secretary (1910), first lord of the Admiralty (1911 and 1939), and chancellor of the exchequer (1924–29). He spent the 1930's in political obscurity, but became prime minister of a coalition government during World War II, rising to greatness and becoming a symbol of the indomitable will to triumph over Nazi Germany. Defeated in the General Election of 1945, he was again elected prime minister in 1951. He wrote extensively, and in 1953 won the Nobel Prize for Literature. He died in 1965, at age 90.

CLEMENTINE HOZIER
(1885–1977)
was born into an upper-class family, but experienced much unhappiness as a young girl when her parents separated. Despite a lack of money, she made a strong impression in social circles with her beauty, intelligence, and charm. In 1908, she married Winston Churchill. She kept their home, bore him five children and proved a loyal support and wise counsel during his very long political career. By nature Clementine was shy and passionate, though she maintained a seemingly cool public persona. In the years of World War II, she undertook the important work of chairing the Red Cross Aid to Russia Appeal, helping to run the Fulmer Chase Maternity Home, and raising funds for the Y.M.C.A. In 1965, she took the title of Baroness Spencer-Churchill of Chartwell. Ill health dogged her old age, but she retained her elegance, independence of mind, and love of family and friends until her death in 1977, at age 92.

She campaigned for him during the General Election of 1922. From Scotland she explained,

> *"I find what people like best is the settlement of the Irish question. So I trot that out and also your share in giving the Boers self-government.... I am exhibiting you as a Cherub Peace Maker with little fluffy wings round your chubby face."*

During the 1930's, Churchill fell into the political wilderness. He spent much of his time at his family home at Chartwell in Kent, painting, writing, and warning Britain of future danger from Nazi Germany. When war did come, Churchill became prime minister. As he later wrote in his memoirs,

> *"I felt as if I were walking with destiny, and that all my past life had been but a preparation for this hour and this trial."*

Throughout the dark years of conflict, Clementine did much in her own right, especially her tireless charity work for Russia. During her visit to the Soviet Union in 1945, Churchill concluded a letter to her,

> *"My darling one I always think of you....Yr personality reaches the gt masses and touches their hearts.*
> *With all my love and constant kisses*
> *I remain your devoted husband*
> *W"*

(It was accompanied by a drawing of a pig, see below.)

Although plagued by ill health in their old age, their last years together were full and rich, and they continued to correspond whenever they were apart. Winston and Clementine's warm union of mind and spirit lasted until Winston's death, at age 90, in 1965. Clementine survived him by 12 years, and died at the age of 92.

Acknowledgments (Text)

LOVE DOWN THE AGES

Section Opener Quote: from *Love: Emotion, Myth and Metaphor* by Robert C. Solomon (Anchor/Doubleday, 1981).
Ovid: *The Fasti, Tristia, Pontic Epistles... of Ovid*, translated by Henry T. Riley (George Bell & Son, London, 1881).
Ovid: The Erotic Poems by Ovid, translated by Peter Green (Penguin Classics, Harmondsworth, 1982). Copyright © Peter Green, 1982. Reproduced by permission of Penguin Books Ltd.
Ovid: A Poet Between Two Worlds by Hermann Frankel (University of California Press, Berkeley and Los Angeles, 1945). Copyright © 1945 Regents of the University of California, renewed © 1973 Hermann Frankel.
Ariwara no Narihira: *Anthology of Japanese Literature* introduced and compiled by Donald Keene (Penguin, Harmondsworth, rev. ed. 1968). [Copyright owner could not be traced.]
The World of the Shining Prince: Court Life in Ancient Japan by Ivan Morris (Oxford University Press, London, 1964). By permission of Oxford University Press.
Pietro Bembo: *The Prettiest Love Letters In the World. Letters between Lucrezia Borgia and Pietro Bembo 1503–1519* translated and prefaced by Hugh Shankland (Collins Harvill, 1987). By permission of HarperCollins Publishers Limited.
Henry IV of France: *Henri IV: Lettres d'amour et écrits politiques* edited by J. P. Babelon (Fayard, Paris, 1988).
John Wilmot, Earl of Rochester: *The Letters of John Wilmot, Earl of Rochester* edited and annotated with an introduction by Jeremy Treglown (Basil Blackwell, Oxford, 1980).
Johann von Goethe: *Letters from Goethe* translated by M. von Herzfeld and C. Melvil Sym (Edinburgh University Press, 1957).
George Bernard Shaw: *Ellen Terry and Bernard Shaw* edited by Christopher St. John (Max Reinhardt, London, 1931).
Theodore Roosevelt, Jr: *Lines of Battle: Letters from American Servicemen, 1941–1945* by Annette Tapert, foreword by David Eisenhower (Times Books, New York, 1987).

PASSIONATE LOVE

Section Opener Quote: from an interview with Marc Chagall, *Newsweek*, April 8, 1985.
Napoleon: *Napoleon's Letters to Josephine 1796–1812* by Henry Foljambe Hall (J.M. Dent, London, 1901).
Beethoven: *The Letters of Beethoven* (3 vols.), edited by Emily Anderson (Macmillan, London, 1961). Reproduced by permission of Macmillan Press Limited. Reprinted from THE LETTERS OF BEETHOVEN by Emily Anderson, with the permission of W. W. Norton & Company, Inc. Copyright © 1961 by Emily Anderson.

Lord Byron: *Byron's Letters and Journals* (12 vols.), edited by Leslie A. Marchand (John Murray, London, 1973/82).
Franz Liszt: *Les plus belles lettres manuscrites de la langue française* by Robert Laffont (Bib. Nat., Paris, 1992).
Victor Hugo: *Victor Hugo* by André Maurois, translated by Gerard Hopkins (Jonathan Cape, London, 1956). Reproduced with permission of Curtis Brown Ltd, London on behalf of the Estate of André Maurois. Copyright the Estate of André Maurois.
Randolph Churchill: *Jennie: Lady Randolph Churchill, a portrait with letters* by Peregrine Churchill and Julia Mitchell (Collins, London, 1974). Copyright © Peregrine S. Churchill. Reproduced by permission of Curtis Brown Ltd, London on behalf of Peregrine S. Churchill.
Henri Gaudier: *Savage Messiah* by H. S. Ede (Gordon Fraser, London, 1971).
Leoš Janáček: *Intimate Letters* edited and translated by John Tyrell (Faber and Faber Limited, London, 1994).
Frida Kahlo: *Frida: a biography of Frida Kahlo* by Hayden Herrera (Bloomsbury, London, 1989).

STAR-CROSSED LOVERS

Section Opener Quote: "Excerpt," from *The Power of Myth* by Joseph Campbell and Bill Moyers. Copyright © 1988 by Apostrophe S. Productions, Inc. and Bill Moyers and Alfred Van der Marck Editions, Inc. for itself and the estate of Joseph Campbell. Used by permission of Doubleday, a division of Bantam Doubleday Dell Publishing Group, Inc.
Heloise: *Abelard and Heloise: The Story of his Misfortunes and The Personal Letters* translated by Betty Radice (The Folio Society, London, 1977).
Catherine of Aragon: *Catherine of Aragon* by Garrett Mattingley (Jonathan Cape, London, 1942).
Robert Emmet: *The Unfortunate Mr. Robert Emmet* by Leon O'Broin (Burns and Oates, London, 1958).
John Keats: *The Letters of John Keats* (2 vols.) edited by Hyder Edward Rollins (Cambridge University Press, 1958).
Peter Withers: *The Fatal Shore* by Robert Hughes (Collins, London, 1987).
Fanny Kemble: *Fanny Kemble* by Dorothy Marshall (Weidenfeld and Nicolson, London, 1977).
Zelda Sayre: *Zelda* by Nancy Milford (The Bodley Head, London 1970).
Franz Kafka: *Franz Kafka, Letters to Milená* edited by Willy Haas and translated by Tania and James Stern (Penguin, Harmondsworth, 1983).

JOYS AND CONSOLATIONS

Section Opener Quote: from "Love and Marriage" by Ernest Havemann, *Life*, September 29, 1961.
Pliny the Younger: *The Letters of the younger Pliny* translated and introduced by Betty Radice (Penguin Classics, Harmondsworth, 1963). Copyright © Betty Radice, 1963, 1969. Reproduced by permission of Penguin Books Ltd.
Mozart: *The Letters of Mozart and his Family* edited by Emily Anderson (Macmillan, London, rev. ed. 1985). Reproduced by permission of Macmillan Press Limited.

Reprinted from THE LETTERS OF MOZART AND HIS FAMILY by Emily Anderson, with the permission of W. W. Norton & Company, Inc. Copyright © 1966 by The Executors of the late Miss Emily Anderson. Copyright © 1985, 1989 by The Macmillan Press.

Matthew Flinders: *Captain Matthew Flinders R.N. his voyages, discoveries and fortunes* by Joseph Bryant (Epworth Press, London, 1928).

John Constable: *John Constable's Correspondence* vol. 6 edited by R. B. Beckett (Suffolk Records Society, Ipswich, 1964).

Sophia Peabody: *Nathaniel Hawthorne and his wife (1884)* by Julia Hawthorne (Archon Books, Hamden, Connecticut, 1968).

Elizabeth Barrett: *The Love Letters of Robert Browning and Elizabeth Barrett* edited and introduced by V. E. Stack (Century, London, 1987).

Anton Chekhov: *The Letters of Anton Pavlovitch Tchehov to Olga Leonardovna Knipper* translated by Constance Garnett (Chatto and Windus, London, 1926). Reproduced by permission of the estate of Constance Garnett and Chatto and Windus.
Letters of Anton Chekhov translated by Michael Henry Heim and Simon Karlinsky (Harper and Row, London, 1973). Copyright © 1973 Harper and Row Publishers, Inc. Reproduced by permission of HarperCollins Publishers.

Robert Peary: *The Noose of Laurels* by Wally Herbert (Grafton, London, 1991).

Winston Churchill: *Clementine Churchill* by Mary Soames (Cassell, London, 1979). Copyright © Mary Soames. Reproduced by permission of Curtis Brown Ltd, London on behalf of Mary Soames.

Every effort has been made by Andromeda Oxford Limited to trace copyright holders where relevant of transcriptions of letters used in this book. Anyone having claims to ownership not identified above is invited to contact Andromeda Oxford Limited.

Further Reading

Letters from Women who Love Too Much: A Closer Look at Relationship Addiction and Recovery by Robin Norwood (Arrow Books, 1988).

The Courtly Love Tradition by Bernard O'Donoghue (Manchester University Press, 1982).

The Faber Book of Letters: Letters written in the English language by Felix Pryor (Faber, London, 1988).

Letter Designs In the Historical Style of the Middle Ages, Illuminated by Muriel Parker (Stemmer House, 1986).

Letters of Jane Austen edited by Lord Brabourne (1884).

Letters of Love: Women Political Prisoners in exile and the Camps edited by J. Voznesenskaya (Quartet Books, 1989).

The Letters of Robert Browning and Elizabeth Barrett Browning 1845–1846 2 vols. edited by E. Kinter (1969).

Love Letters: an Illustrated Anthology by Antonia Fraser (Barrie and Jenkins, London, 1976, 1989).

On Love by Stendahl, translated by Vyvyan Holland (Chatto and Windus, London, 1928).

The Psychology of Love edited by Robert J. Sternberg and Michael L. Barnes (Yale University Press, Newhaven, 1988).

Roman Marriage by Susan Treggiari (Clarendon Press, Oxford, 1991).

Romantic Correspondence: Women, Politics and the Fiction of Letters by Mary A. Favret (Cambridge University Press).

Romantic Love by Susan S. Hendrich and Clyde Hendrick (Sage Publications, Newbury Park, California, 1992).

Second Treasury of the World's Greatest Letters by Wallace Brockway and Bart Keith Winer (1950)

A Treasury of the World's Greatest Letters from Ancient Days to Our Time by M. Lincoln Schuster (Simon and Schuster, New York, 1948).

800 Years of Women's Letters by Olga Kenyon and P. D. James (Alan Sutton, Stroud, U.K.).

Credits (Illustrations)

Preussischer Kulturbesitz, Musikabteilung mit Mendelssohn-Archiv **51t** H C Robbins Landon, France **51b** Bayer Staatsbibliothek, Munich **52cl** H C Robbins Landon, France **52bl** H C Robbins Landon, France **52br** H C Robbins Landon, France **52–53** Historisches Museum der Stadt Wien **54** Miami University Art Museum, Oxford, Ohio, gift of Dr Jonathan S Bishop **54–55** Comune di Ravenna, Biblioteca Classense, Italy **55** Comune di Ravenna, Biblioteca Classense, Italy **56** AOL/Giorgio Biserni **57** By courtesy of the National Portrait Gallery, London **58** Bulloz, Paris **59c** BAL/ Giraudon **59r** BN **60** RHPL/Philip Craven **61bl** AKG **61br** SWK **62t** MVP **62b** BN **63t** MVP **63b** BN **64** Bulloz **65t** MVP **65bl** BN **65br** MVP **66t** National Trust Photographic Library/Derrick E Witty **66b** Chartwell College/Curtis Brown **67** Courtesy His Grace the Duke of Marlborough/Blenheim Palace, Oxford **68t** BAL/Tate Gallery **68c** Chartwell College/Curtis Brown **69** Oxford Picture Library/Chris Andrews **71l** Albert Sloman Library, University of Essex **72** Musee National D'Art Moderne, Centre Georges Pompidou, Paris **73** Tate Gallery Publications, London **74** Moravian Regional Museum, Czech Republic **74–75** Moravian Regional Museum, Czech Republic **75** Moravian Regional Museum, Czech Republic **76l** Lebrecht Collection, London **76r** Courtesy John Tyrrell, Nottingham **77** Lebrecht Collection **79** Instituto Nacional de Bellas Artes Y Literatura/Gelman Collection/Centro Cultural Arte Contemporaneo A.C., Mexico **80** Courtesy of Emmy Lou Packard **80–81** Instituto Nacional de Bellas Artes Y Literatura/Gelman Collection/Centro Cultural Arte Contemporaneo A.C., Mexico **84** Giraudon, Paris **85** BN **86** BAL/British Library **87** AOL/Robert Polidori **88t** BAL/Kunsthistorisches Museum, Vienna **88b** Bodleian Library, Oxford **89** BAL/Walker Art Gallery, Liverpool **90** V & A **90–91** The College of Arms, London **91** S **92** National Gallery of Ireland **93tl** National Library of Ireland **93tr** Irish State Paper Office **93b** HDC **95** National Library of Ireland **96** Fitzwilliam Museum, Cambridge **97t and 97c** Keith Wynn/Photo Craft (Hampstead) Ltd/Reproduced by permission of the London Borough of Camden from the Collections at Keats House, Hampstead **97r** Charles Roberts Autograph Letters Collection, Haverford College Library **98** AOL/Ian Fraser **99br and 99bl** Keith Wynn/Photo Craft (Hampstead) Ltd/Reproduced by permission of the London Borough of Camden from the Collections at Keats House, Hampstead **101t** University of Reading, Rural History Centre **101c** Wiltshire Archaeological and Natural History Society, Devizes **101b** AOL/Derek Parker/Wiltshire Records Office, Trowbridge **102t** AOL/David O'Brien/The Royal Wiltshire Yeomanry **102b** Archives Office of Tasmania **103** Tasmanian Museum and Art Gallery **104l** The Historical Society of Pennsylvania **104r** M & M **105t** Courtesy of the Pennsylvania Academy of the Fine Arts, Philadelphia. Bequest of Henry C. Carey (The Carey Collection) **105b** Collection Mrs Roy Plomley **106t** The Historical Society of Pennsylvania **106b** Courtesy, Georgia Department of Archives and History **107** By courtesy of the National Portrait Gallery, London **108–109** Princeton University Libraries **110–111** Princeton University Libraries **112** Archiv Klaus Wagenbach, Berlin **113** Archiv Klaus Wagenbach, Berlin **114** Archiv Klaus Wagenbach, Berlin **114–115** RHPL **118l** British Museum, London **118r** British Museum, London **119** BAL/Metropolitan Museum of Art **120l** The Pierpoint Morgan Library 1994 **120tr** Z **120br** Mauro Pucciarelli **122l** ISM, Library **122r** Hunterian Museum & Art Gallery, University of Glasgow **123t** ISM, Mozarts Geburtshaus **123bl** British Library, London **123br** British Library, London **124t** Kunsthistorisches Museum, Vienna **125tl** ISM, Mozarts Geburtshaus **125tr** ISM, Mozarts Geburtshaus **126tl** National Maritime Museum, Greenwich **126tr** By courtesy of the National Portrait Gallery, London **126–127** British Library, London **127** The Subdeanery, Lincoln **128** National Maritime Museum, Greenwich **128–129** Lincoln City Council **130t** Tate Gallery Publications, London **130b** Private Collection/David O'Brien **131t** Tate Gallery Publications, London **131b** Merseyside County Art Galleries **132–133** 1942.9.10.(606)/PA: Constable, John, Wivenhoe Park, Essex, Widener Collection © 1994 Board of Trustees, National Gallery of Art, Washington **133** Private Collection/A C Cooper Ltd **134r** Courtesy Peabody Essex Museum, Salem, Massachusetts **134l** Henry W and Albert A Berg Collection, The New York Public Library, Astor, Lenox and Tilden Foundations **135t** Courtesy Peabody Essex Museum, Salem, Massachusetts **137** Lightdance Photography **137 inset** Concord Free Public Library, Massachusetts **138t** The Provost and Fellows, Eton College **138–139** Wellesley College Library, Special Collections/John Murray Publishers Ltd **139** Fitzwilliam Museum, Cambridge **140t** Westminster City Archives, London **140bl** Wellesley College Library, Special Collections/John Murray Publishers Ltd **140br** Corporation of London, Greater London Record Office **141** **142** AOL **143** Novosti, London **144–145** Novosti, London **146t** Abplanalp Library, Westbrook College **147c** Library of Congress **147br** National Archives and Records Administration, Center for Polar Archives **148–149** B & C Alexander, Dorset **149** Abplanalp Library, Westbrook College **150r** HDC **150l** Spencer Churchill Papers/Curtis Brown **151** Courtesy Lady Mary Soames, DBE/Cecil Beaton Archives **152t** Spencer Churchill Papers/Churchill Archives Centre **152b** Courtesy Lady Mary Soames, DBE **152-3** Chartwell College/Curtis Brown **153** Spencer Churchill Papers/Curtis Brown

Project Editor Vicky Egan
Editors Fiona Mullan, Mike Brown, Pamela Egan
Art Editor Chris Munday
Designers Frankie Wood, Jerry Goldie
Picture Research Manager Jo Rapley
Picture Researchers Celia Dearing, Suzanne Williams, David Pratt
Researchers Ann Furtado, Helen McCurdy, Lin Thomas
Indexer Mike March
Proofreader Lin Thomas
Editorial Assistant Niki Moores
Project Manager Graham Bateman
Production Clive Sparling, David Archer

For Reader's Digest
Executive Editor James Wagenvoord
Editorial Director Deborah DeFord
Art & Design Director Michele Italiano-Perla
Managing Editors Diane Shanley, Christine Molson
Editorial Associate Daniela Marchetti

Andromeda Oxford Limited would like to thank Claire Turner for her administrative support; and Andrew Hoddinott at the School of Oriental and African Studies. Color origination by Eray Scan pte Ltd., Singapore.

Index

Page numbers in **bold** indicate main entry on writer and recipient of featured letter. Page numbers in *italic* indicate a reference in a picture caption.